The Renaissance

An Enthralling Guide to a Period of Rebirth in Arts, Science and Culture

© Copyright 2023 - All rights reserved.

The content contained within this book may not be reproduced, duplicated, or transmitted without direct written permission from the author or the publisher.

Under no circumstances will any blame or legal responsibility be held against the publisher, or author, for any damages, reparation, or monetary loss due to the information contained within this book, either directly or indirectly.

Legal Notice:

This book is copyright protected. It is only for personal use. You cannot amend, distribute, sell, use, quote, or paraphrase any part, or the content within this book, without the consent of the author or publisher.

Disclaimer Notice:

Please note the information contained within this document is for educational and entertainment purposes only. All effort has been executed to present accurate, up-to-date, reliable, and complete information. No warranties of any kind are declared or implied. Readers acknowledge that the author is not engaging in the rendering of legal, financial, medical, or professional advice. The content within this book has been derived from various sources. Please consult a licensed professional before attempting any techniques outlined in this book.

By reading this document, the reader agrees that under no circumstances is the author responsible for any losses, direct or indirect, that are incurred as a result of the use of the information contained within this document, including, but not limited to, errors, omissions, or inaccuracies.

Free limited time bonus

Stop for a moment. We have a free bonus set up for you. The problem is this: we forget 90% of everything that we read after 7 days. Crazy fact, right? Here's the solution: we've created a printable, 1-page pdf summary for this book that you're reading now. All you have to do to get your free pdf summary is to go to the following website:

https://livetolearn.lpages.co/enthrallinghistory/

Once you do, it will be intuitive. Enjoy, and thank you!

Table of Contents

INTRODUCTION 1
CHAPTER ONE – PRE-RENAISSANCE EUROPE...4
CHAPTER TWO – THE BIRTH OF REBIRTH 13
CHAPTER THREE – THE ESSENCE OF THE RENAISSANCE.......................20
CHAPTER FOUR – ITALIAN RENAISSANCE ART 24
CHAPTER FIVE – RENAISSANCE SCIENCE AND TECHNOLOGY..............58
CHAPTER SIX – THE NORTHERN RENAISSANCE..64
CHAPTER SEVEN – THE END OF THE RENAISSANCE 78
CONCLUSION 84
HERE'S ANOTHER BOOK BY ENTHRALLING HISTORY THAT
YOU MIGHT LIKE..86
FREE LIMITED TIME BONUS..87
SOURCES...88

Introduction

Today, most curious people know of the Renaissance, at least through the amazing artistic works of Leonardo da Vinci and Michelangelo. Perhaps this is to be expected, as the paintings, sculptures, and architecture of the Renaissance never fail to dazzle viewers lucky enough to experience them in person. Indeed, visual art is one of the most iconic parts of the period in Medieval Europe we now refer to as the Renaissance, but there is so much more to unpack within the movement that one might even get overwhelmed. The Renaissance is comprised of various aspects, all carefully correlated with each other, that together produced one of the most prosperous, intellectually profound, and aesthetically pleasing periods in the history of Europe. This book aims to cover this period by unpacking every detail that made it what it is today and by analyzing the causes and consequences of the Renaissance.

    The Renaissance, or "rebirth," is a fitting name since it entailed a complete re-imagination of European civilization, an awakening from a deep slumber of ideological, technological, and moral stagnation and uncertainty. A full rebirth of what "Europe" stood for did take place, though perhaps unknowingly for many people. Though the Renaissance today is seen as the continent's strive towards progress, it manifested itself most clearly in the upper echelons of European society, while the lives of the poorest were hardly, if at all, affected. Still, after the chaos that beset Europe after the collapse of the Western Roman Empire—the main pillar of civilization and stability of the continent for hundreds of years—it is the Renaissance that is credited with recovering European civilization and setting it back on the right track from the depths of the

Dark Ages that immediately followed the fall of Rome. Renaissance thinkers bridged their time with the long-lost or forgotten knowledge of the ancient world, the ancient Greeks and Romans, that was full of glory and stability and displayed man as the center of the world. What made the Renaissance so special was that it recognized this, skipping the ideological vacuum that had emerged in the post-Roman world caused by the migration of new peoples, the destruction of old power structures, and the establishment of Christianity as the new moral center of the world.

Ultimately, this rebirth was concerned with more than European values and putting man back on center stage. It was also an age of unparalleled scientific progress, accelerated by the diffusion of knowledge from the East and the constant desire to learn more and grow one's horizons. New discoveries and theories shocked the state of the world and people's understanding of it. The theories of Copernicus, a Polish astronomer and mathematician, challenged the geocentric model of the Earth accepted for ages, which saw the Earth as the center of the universe. Instead, Copernicus mathematically proved that it was, in fact, the Earth and the planets that moved around the Sun—something that was, at first, vehemently condemned by those to whom it posed the most danger—the leaders of the Catholic Church. In the 16th century, Italian scientist Galileo Galilei contributed much to our understanding of the natural world, laying the foundations for what would eventually become the revered scientific method, perfecting the telescope, and finding more evidence for the heliocentric world. These and many other scientific and mathematical novelties accelerated the Renaissance and gave it new meaning. Man was placed at the center of attention and made curious and capable of overcoming difficulties, whether through his virtues or science and learning.

This book seeks to tell the history of the Renaissance—arguably one of the most influential periods in world history—that transformed European material and immaterial life, opening new avenues of thought, ideology, and exploration. The first chapter of the book will serve as an introduction, summarizing the state of pre-Renaissance Europe to provide a better context for the developments that increasingly took place after the late 13th century. Then, the middle of the book will cover different major developments of the Renaissance, whether political, social, or economic, that shaped the continent. We will look at some of the biggest Renaissance names, like the infamous Medici family of

Florence, great artists like Raphael and Botticelli, thinkers like Erasmus and Luther, scientists like Galileo, and many others who influenced the movement and helped it become what it is remembered as now. By looking at some of the most important breakthroughs in thought and technology, we will contrast Renaissance Europe with Europe of the Middle Ages. Finally, the book will conclude by assessing the bigger impact of the Renaissance on the continent's history and the sociopolitical dynamics that would unfold after the late 16th century.

Chapter One – Pre-Renaissance Europe

The Fall of Rome

Ancient Rome deservedly occupies a place among the most important civilizations in history. From 8th century B.C. to the 5th century A.D., the history of what we refer to as ancient Rome is full of exciting developments that still exert their influence today—for example, by the sheer scale of the material cultural heritage that exists in the ruins of once-great Rome. Transitioning from a kingdom to a republic to an empire, the state that grew out of the Italian Peninsula at its height incorporated all of Western Europe, North Africa, England, much of the Balkans and Anatolia, and the Levant. Rome was the greatest empire in the known world by a huge margin, excelling not only in warfare but also in statecraft—creating one of the most iconic forms of government to this day, built on the principles of republicanism. To put things into perspective, while the Romans exercised control over territories hundreds of miles away from the great city of Rome through a network of carefully-designed bureaucracy, northern, central, and eastern Europe were still tribal and sometimes nomadic. These peoples, referred to as barbarians by the Romans, were scattered around the dense forests of the European continent. They constantly struggled against the Roman legions, who sought to take over their lands and bring "civilization" and the Pax Romana—the Roman Peace—to them.

By the final days of the Roman Empire, the notion of Pax Romana had become internalized into the consciousness of the empire's subjects. Roman society was very hierarchical and clearly stratified, and most people living in the empire were not considered Roman citizens until very late. Still, Rome had a sense of grandeur and might it still exerts today to some extent. Though constantly involved in economic, military, and political troubles, the empire symbolized stability, victory, and peace. Due to its adherence to republicanism and civil law, the Roman Empire inspired many people, including commoners, who at least could compare their lives to the lives of barbarian "savages." Roman citizens were part of a huge, interconnected world and cherished this fact, though most were less privileged than others. During the heyday of the Roman Empire, it seemed like the empire would last forever, constantly expanding and civilizing the rest of the known world.

However, all empires eventually fall, and Rome is perhaps the clearest example. Over time, the sheer size of the empire became practically unmanageable. We must remember that Romans administered very remote provinces in an age when the most effective method of communication was sending messengers on horseback from one place to another. This could sometimes take weeks or even months and was associated with a myriad of problems, even if the Romans managed to build a cohesive network of roads to connect their domains. Eventually, it became clear that Britannia or Syria, for example, could not be simply governed from Rome. So, the administrative system of the empire became more and more decentralized, giving more and more power to locally-appointed governors. Constant clashes with barbarians or upset local populations increased interdependence between the governors and the Roman legions, undoubtedly the most professional and strongest in the world at the time. This meant that power became fragmented, and the Roman Senate—the republican governmental body of the empire—could no longer effectively exercise its direct influence. This is, eventually, how Rome went from an empire to a republic. The rise of powerful individuals, often commanders with many loyal legions, could hardly be contested. A system built on deliberation, public discourse, and the prevention of dictatorships collapsed. The Senate still held some legislative power, but the real power lay in the hands of the emperors.

When the emperors were wise and capable of governance, Rome experienced few problems. In fact, the reign of the "five good emperors" from the end of the 1st century to the late 2nd century is considered one of the most prosperous times of ancient Roman civilization. However, if the individual emperors could not cut it and were unsuited to rule—perhaps too distracted or simply drunk—holding such a massive empire together was practically impossible. This resulted in many civil wars in which different commanders fought each other for power and influence in the state, while the Senate always plotted from behind the scenes to install whomever it saw most fit to rule. To fix the problem, the empire was divided in the 4th century into the Western and Eastern Roman Empires. Eastern Rome, with its new capital at Constantinople, was richer and more prosperous than its Western counterpart. Though governed by the Romans, the Eastern Roman Empire was essentially based on the social and cultural heritage of ancient Greece, the old Hellenistic world that included the Balkans, Anatolia, Syria, Palestine, and Egypt. It was distinct from the Latin Western Roman Empire (culturally, above all) and had fewer political struggles.

The Western Roman Empire, on the other hand, was a dying state from the day it was formally separated from the East. Victim to constant civil wars, barbarian invasions, and economic troubles, it lacked effective administration to keep it together. The situation got worse in the 5th century, when the great migration of people from the east altered the demographic state of Europe, forcing many barbarians, who had previously lived at the peripheries of the empire, to flock into its borders. Hundreds of thousands of people migrated from the east to the west, and Roman legions could not stop them from entering the borders of Rome. They settled in Germany, France, northern Italy, Iberia, and Britain, and their migration was not exactly peaceful. Vandals, Goths, and Anglo-Saxons overwhelmed Roman armies, while the Asian Huns, ferocious warriors on horseback who had caused the great migration of European people, decimated the Roman countryside, and pillaged the land.

The result was the fall of the Western Roman Empire in 476 A.D., when the last Roman Emperor, Romulus Augustus, was overthrown by the Germanic king of the barbarians, Odoacer, who declared himself the ruler of Italy. The rest of the empire, already quite decentralized, was quickly seized by different barbarian forces. Visigoths (Western Goths) established their own kingdom in Iberia and the southern part of the old Roman province of Gaul. Vandals, whose atrocities during the sack of Rome in 455 gave the word "vandalism" its meaning, occupied much of the North African coast. Northern Gaul and most of modern-day Germany were divided by the Franks, Saxons, Alamanni, Frisians, and Thuringians, while the British Isles were invaded by the Angles, Saxons, and Jutes. While the Eastern Roman Empire would continue to exist for another thousand years, these peoples took over the ruins of the old Western Roman Empire and founded their own kingdoms (though, in the beginning, their hold over the territories was just as superficial and lacked political structures). The fall of Rome in 476 ushered in a new period we now call the Middle Ages—about a millennium of chaos and uncertainty in which Western Europe tried to stabilize and find its identity, which was lost with the collapse of the Western Roman Empire.

Post-Roman Europe

Post-Roman Europe was drastically different. The power vacuum created by the collapse of the Western Roman Empire needed to be filled, but the barbarians who had just arrived and set up kingdoms in old Roman territories were by no means advanced societies. They objectively lacked the level of sophistication the ancient Roman and Greek civilizations were known for. Though they had complex belief systems, their organization was largely tribal, and their hierarchy depended on relationships between war chiefs and their subjects. Many barbarians marveled at the heritage the Romans had left (as in the British Isles), attributing them to the works of mythical creatures like giants, as they were unaware of the Roman civilization and its merits. The overwhelming majority of society was illiterate, with no real incentive to study and learn. Admittedly, barbarians knew how to fight, but they did not exactly know what to do when they were not fighting. Confusion and uncertainty beset the European continent. We must remember that many commoners who inhabited different provinces in Gaul, Iberia, or Italy had experienced both Roman and barbarian rule but did not know with whom their allegiance lay. Were they to look at Rome, now under Odoacer and his successors—before they were eventually replaced by other warring barbarian dynasties—or were they to look at the newly emergent "kings" of their territories?

Immediately after the fall of Rome, as the political organization of the continent was still adjusting, two centers of influence emerged. At first glance, they seemed to emerge as potential successors of the stability previously provided by the Roman Empire. One, obviously, was the Eastern Roman Empire, also known as the Byzantine Empire—a name that stems from the great city of Byzantium (Constantinople), which claimed to be the true successor of the Roman traditions and way of life. Constantinople had long eclipsed Rome as the greatest city in Europe and was reaching its prime around the time Rome was being sacked by the Vandals. Combining Roman governance and administration with its Hellenistic traditions and heritage, the Eastern Roman Empire was the largest and the richest power in Europe. Its inhabitants had also been affected much less by the great migration than the rest of Europe. It was a thriving society, much more stable and peaceful than whatever the rest of the post-Roman world could offer, though it did have its own problems. In the beginning, the Byzantine Empire seemed interested in emerging as the new pillar of stability, and barbarian kings sometimes declared their allegiance to the emperor in Constantinople. Emperor Justinian, for example, one of the most successful Byzantine emperors, managed to reconquer a significant part of the old Western Roman Empire, with his legions taking over much of Italy, North Africa, and Iberia in the 6th century. Constantinople seemed ready to offer "mandates" to new kings in return for their cooperation or allegiance to help legitimize them in the eyes of the population.

However, as time passed, it became clear that Byzantium could not provide a suitable alternative for the rest of post-Roman Europe. The main problem was that it was too far away from the new barbarian kingdoms, many of which were simply uninterested in basing the source of their power in such a far-away realm. Yes, perhaps in the eyes of the population, formal or informal connection with Constantinople meant something, but it yielded no practical results toward the consolidation of power and establishment of new dynasties. New kingdoms could not be dependent on some artificial relationship with Constantinople. This was even more apparent once the Eastern Roman Empire became culturally distinct from the West. Latin was replaced with Greek, and old Roman deities and symbolism were gradually left out in favor of Hellenism. Constantinople looked increasingly to the east instead of the west, especially as Justinian's gains were slowly lost. Grabbing onto the barbarian West was simply unnecessary when the empire had many of its own problems.

The second alternative, the one that eventually triumphed over the option of Byzantium, was none other than the Roman Catholic Church. Christianity had become the official religion of the Roman Empire in 313 with the Edict of Milan, and though it had made quite a bit of progress in supplanting different religions in Roman territories to emerge as the sole most dominant one, the fall of Rome in 476. hindered that process. Still, by the time new barbarian kingdoms were establishing themselves in place of the old Roman domains, the Catholic Church, headquartered in Rome, also vied for influence, seeking to Christianize the new barbarian kings and complete the process of making Europe fully Christian.

A complicated dynamic soon emerged. As the new kings sought to absorb old Roman structures and Romanize themselves to appear more glorious or prosperous to their subjects and gain more legitimacy, they stumbled upon Christianity, which, for them, symbolized the might of the old Roman Empire. This was especially so because Byzantium was also Christian, and the East-West Schism had still not officially occurred. The bishopric of Rome, the most prestigious alongside the bishoprics of Constantinople, Jerusalem, Antioch, and Alexandria, thus started to form informal alliances with the new barbarian rulers, who increasingly became Christian. Since their societies were heavily dependent on the actions of their ruler, owing to the old tribal chief loyalty, they followed the lead of their kings and adopted Christianity. In that way, they could get another Christian "mandate" to legitimize themselves. If the bishop of Rome recognized their kingship and accepted them as Christian kings, then surely they were worthy of being the successors of the great Roman Empire, though what that meant was still unclear.

The role of Christianity in Europe was amplified with the emergence of a new, soon-to-be rival religion in the Arab world known as Islam. Spreading like wildfire, Islam took the Middle East and North Africa by storm, as devoted Arab warriors went on jihads to spread the religion throughout the world, creating significant problems for Byzantium. By the 8th century, they had taken over much of the Levant, Persia, Egypt, and Carthage, destroying the kingdom of the Vandals and expanding into Iberia, whose recently Christianized Visigoth kings were almost fully wiped out. Eventually, Muslim incursions were ended by the Franks at the Battle of Poitiers in 732, commanded by Charles Martel, but most of Iberia would remain Muslim for many centuries to come.

The emergence of Islam and its rapid expansion was a unifying factor for the Christian Church in Rome and the new barbarian kingdoms of Europe, who embraced Christianity and gained the favor of the bishop of Rome—the pope. Most importantly, Charlemagne the Great, king of the Franks and the man who would conquer half of Europe in the late 8th century, received special papal approval. Forcing the Germanic tribes to convert to Christianity after decades of waging war and extending the borders of his realms to include most of modern-day France, the western half of Germany, and northern Italy, Charlemagne was a devout Christian and often generous to the pope. Eventually, in the year 800, Pope Leo III crowned him the Holy Roman Emperor at St. Peter's Cathedral in Rome, essentially making him the new suzerain of Europe on par with the emperor in the East.

Charlemagne's triumphs and his successful Carolingian dynasty asserted the dominance of the Roman Catholic Church as the undisputed central institution of post-Roman Europe by the year 1000. As time passed, new kingdoms and principalities emerged from the chaos of the post-Roman world, synthesizing new values of Catholic Christianity with the feudal system. Christianity overwhelmingly dominated the cultures of new state-like formations, with the pope as the most respected authority. The system that eventually emerged from the Early Middle Ages sought to stabilize the problems that had arisen after the fall of the Roman Empire.

Dark Ages

The Early Middle Ages is, largely speaking, the stereotypical "medieval" period depicted in today's culture and embedded in the consciousness of many people. It was a time when the sharp hierarchical divisions of Europe were still being institutionalized, those that would remain unchanged for hundreds of years. All the power was concentrated either in feudal lords, barons, dukes, and kings or in Catholic religious authorities, who held much influence over the political figures. The overwhelming majority of the population lived in terrible daily conditions, dependent on good harvests and the will of their suzerains. Constant wars and raids often decimated the countryside. And though the overall political structure of the western half of the continent was slowly stabilizing, most people's everyday lives were by no means peaceful. Literacy rates were horrendously low, with only the clergy and the members of the highest class being educated. Cities and towns were small, centered mostly around marketplaces.

In addition to generally uninteresting, repetitive, and harsh living conditions, the Early Middle Ages can also be characterized by a cultural and ideological uniformity, the likes of which was perhaps never again present in Europe. After the fall of the Roman Empire, especially after the year 1000, Christianity stood proudly at the center of everything

European. This was largely because the Church viewed itself as the unifying force of Europe—something that was true to an extent. This, in turn, resulted in the clergy emerging as among the most universally respected and authoritative figures to the members of the high and low classes of society. Devotion to a truly Christian way of life was considered the most noble and virtuous thing a person could practice since attaining salvation was supposed to be the objective of every Christian. People would go to great lengths for this—going on distant pilgrimages and donating to the Church were among the best and most common things done by the people who could afford them. The role of the Church and Christianity was reconfirmed with the era of the Crusades—the 200-year struggle of European Christendom to conquer the Holy Land of Jerusalem and its surrounding areas from its Muslim rulers. In the eight main campaigns that began in 1095, tens of thousands of Christians died fighting in the name of Christ. But Christendom could not achieve any long-lasting victories in the Levant, forced to eventually abandon its gains.

Still, the Crusades reconfirmed papal authority and became a very prestigious endeavor during the 12th and 13th centuries. It was implied that devoted rulers would campaign to the Holy Land if Rome called a crusade, and success in the campaigns was associated with great honor and dignity. The Crusades also helped to fully separate the Western Catholic Church of Rome from the Eastern Orthodox Church, with its head being the patriarch of Constantinople. The differences that stemmed from the cultural variation between the West and the Byzantine Empire eventually escalated further and further, resulting in issues between the two camps regarding the interpretation of Christian doctrines and scriptures. In the 11th century, the patriarch of Constantinople was excommunicated from the Church by the pope, and the Eastern Church officially separated from the Western Church. In 1204, during the infamous Fourth Crusade, a group of European Crusaders changed their course and unexpectedly sacked Constantinople, though they had been headed to the Holy Land. This put an irreparable strain on the relations of the Eastern and Western Church.

An important development right before the beginning of the Renaissance was the almost doubling of Europe's population between the years 1000 and 1300, peaking at about seventy-five million people. Europe's rapid population growth owed itself to the relative stabilization of affairs after the chaos of the collapse of the Roman Empire. However, by the mid-14th century, at least a third of the European population died due to the Black Death epidemic, setting back progress considerably. Spreading from Asia, the bubonic plague ravaged Europe, with its victims dying either shortly after contracting the disease or after suffering long and gruesome deaths. Urban areas experienced rapid depopulation, and the labor shortage caused by the epidemic triggered even further damage. Population levels would not be the same until about 1550.

The bubonic plague exposed Europe to its main problem—the continent was perpetually vulnerable to large-scale disease outbreaks, unable to combat them due to a lack of medicine. The poor folk particularly suffered from the diseases, vehemently praying to God they could avoid the misfortune, but to no avail. The plague set back Europe's development for who knows how many years. Life expectancy declined considerably. About a fifth of all newborns would die before they could live for even one year.

This, combined with constant wars between states and the ideological and cultural standstill of Middle Ages Europe, resulted in this period being deemed the "Dark Ages." However, this term was not applied to the period until much later, when the succeeding periods resulted in progress, learning, and relative prosperity compared to the misery of the Dark Ages. In fact, it is quite surprising that, not even two hundred years after it had been decimated by the plague, Europe would be a completely new place. Instead of empty, rat-infested, dirty, and muddy streets of European towns, clean, paved roads would emerge, often full of people. The development of new professions would encourage the regrowth of urban areas. High society would thrive as the rediscoveries of ancient texts would awaken a long-lost European culture, one that had remained unknown for about a thousand years. Scientific and technological progress would greatly improve the quality of all aspects of life and lead to a new drive to learn, explore the world, and grow as human beings. In short, after centuries of stagnation and idleness, Europe was primed for a rebirth.

Chapter Two – The Birth of Rebirth

Entering the Renaissance

As mentioned, European towns and cities grew rapidly in size and population during the 12th and 13th centuries. This was largely due to the level of sovereignty these cities experienced compared to France or England. Due to the complex nature of the Holy Roman Empire (composed of hundreds of individual free cities), for example, baronies, provinces, and other administrative groups were very decentralized, though formally ruled by an emperor. This meant that individual entities had more freedom and were constantly competing with one another. This was especially true for ones in Germany, the Low Countries, and Northern Italy.

In the Low Countries, cities benefitted from being close to a coast at the crossroads of northern trade routes. Due to the lack of centralized Italian states, many different city-states had also popped up in Italy, much as in ancient Greece. These city-states, while all "Italian," were ruled by different rulers and constantly competing with each other. Urban growth was most prevalent in these areas because of this. Since these cities were not supported from outside—as, say, smaller towns in France or England would have been tied economically or administratively to the rest of the king's realms—many different institutions and services, such as hospitals, universities, or guilds, were concentrated together.

Urban growth and the decentralized city-state structures of Europe can certainly be considered a prerequisite of the Renaissance. In Northern Italy, where the most marvelous achievements of the Renaissance took place and from where the movement originated, for example, there were about twenty city-states by the 14th century.

We must remember that the movement or period we now call the Renaissance was not separate, broken off from the Middle Ages from the beginning. Rather, the developments took place gradually and simultaneously from about 1350 to 1530, centered in Italy and then spreading to the rest of the continent. The Renaissance was a combination of artistic, intellectual, scientific, socio-political, and technological progress that transformed how Europeans viewed life and affected the continent and the world for generations to come. Urban growth and the increased interconnectedness of different regions of the continent by the 14th century was a huge benefactor to kick-starting the process.

The Italian Peninsula, situated conveniently at a crossroads between the rest of Europe and the eastern world across the Mediterranean, was a perfect place for the cultural and material exchange about to take place. Thanks to the expansion of trade and commerce in the 12th century, several Italian city-states became very prosperous and could hold their own against bigger empires. Venice and Genoa, for example, were powerful trading empires, basing their power on their maritime capabilities. The pope controlled Rome and its surrounding areas, and the Kingdom of Naples held the south, while Florence and Milan were among the most influential city-states in Northern Italy. Social divisions did exist, but despite their diverse lifestyles, they were all interconnected. These urban relationships had only existed on this scale during the height of the Roman Empire, when city councils, courts, and public gathering areas were greatly organized and looked after. Moreover, Italy was where Roman heritage was most visible—in the most literal sense of the world—something that made the inhabitants of the city-states proud.

One way the Italians consciously reconnected with their Roman ancestors was through the political organization of their city-states. From about the 13th century, most Italian city-states were republics ruled by popular assemblies. The size and nature of the assemblies varied, but they were very similar to ancient Roman rule since they were usually comprised of wealthy male elites. Participation in public life was regarded as an honor, so there were clear distinctions between who was fit to rule and who wasn't (though that did not mean social mobility was impossible). Wealthy merchants, for example, were as influential as the nobility, though they may not have held as much land. The bulk of the urban population was made up of local artisans and shopkeepers specializing in this or that industry and contributing their lot to the thriving scene of the city. This kind of social division also reflected the ancient Roman patrician-plebeian divide.

Still, political life was just as dynamic. Powerful families of the Italian city-states often had conflicting interests, vying for power from different sources and competing to emerge dominant. Some city-states would descend into outright hereditary rule because of this. For example, the Visconti family had become the most powerful in Milan, thanks to its huge textile manufacturing business, but would be overthrown in the year 1447 by the Sforza family, which imposed its own despotic rule on the city for years. The infamous Medici family, on the other hand, managed to become hereditary rulers of Florence, building up their fortune by monopolizing the banking industry. By contrast, the Republic of Venice was about as republican as it could get. Its ruler—the doge—was elected by a popular assembly, the Senate, and held executive powers that would be balanced by the Great Council and the Senate. This system of checks and balances, while not exactly resulting in the representative democracy that is the most common form of governance today, was nevertheless a rarity in the medieval world. It stemmed partly from the cultural and intellectual novelties and rediscoveries we will cover later. In part, it represented those rediscoveries and novelties by replicating the type of polity preferred by the ancient Romans.

The New Cultural Center of Europe

It is not surprising that Florence is considered the cradle of the Italian Renaissance, from which all other developments of the movement occurred in later stages. It is the city most associated with the Renaissance even to this day, and several factors contributed to its emergence as the new cultural center of Western Europe. The city-state underwent tremendous economic and cultural growth from the 13th to the 16th centuries, and all of the factors played complementary roles in Florence's meteoric rise.

Located in the northern part of the Italian Peninsula in the province of Tuscany, Florence was a modest city on the Arno River after the collapse of the Roman Empire. It experienced similar levels of instability as other places in that part of the world for the first 500 years or so after the fall of Rome. Still, its convenient location and smart governance eventually combined to make it one of the most prosperous cities in Europe. Ruled by wealthy merchants, known as the *grandi*, Florence accrued considerable wealth that its rulers poured into the city's development. The *grandi* commissioned artisans, architects, and craftsmen to upgrade their own estates, which were close to the city or inside its walls, and so contributed to making Florence look good, as well. Government officials were elected from several merchant guilds, so the power stayed in that class. It was a typical oligarchy, where the means of power was in the hands of a few rich individuals. These, in combination with lawyers and city militia, enforced the laws and conducted foreign affairs. Popular councils also convened to discuss civic matters, again building on the traditions embedded in the consciousness of many from ancient Roman times.

In the 14th century, hardships fell on Florence and the rest of the continent due to the spread of the Black Death. The city's lower classes revolted in the Ciompi uprising, pressuring the elites and demanding more economic and social equality. This led to a rather turbulent period in the history of Florence that would partially end about 1434 when Cosimo de' Medici and his family emerged at the top of Florentine politics. One of the richest families in Italy by that point, drawing its wealth from overseeing one of the most efficient banking systems, the Medici gained the loyalty of the city's militia and overthrew the other rulers. This move was partially motivated by the family's will to expand its influence and wealth, and both goals were successfully reached. Then, through the manipulation of the electoral system in place, Cosimo de' Medici took control of the most important offices of the government and emerged as essentially the sole ruler of the prosperous city-state.

The tenure of the Medici further accelerated Florence's rise to power. In 1406, the city-state conquered the neighboring city-state of Pisa, extending its control and territories and possessing another rather rich city. The Medici capitalized on this gain—control of Pisa gave them direct access to the sea, through which they grew their wealth. Textile manufacturing and commerce thrived in the city, and knowing that the Medici were to be their patrons, more and more people flowed in. By the mid-15th century, the city had become one of the most urbanized areas in Europe. High levels of urbanization had ripple effects in other aspects of life—most prominently on literacy rates. Numerous new schools and universities were constructed, creating a more competent workforce that boosted the income of the city and the development of very well-cultured, tasteful, and proud citizens. In other words, all the pre-requisites for the great cultural advancements that were to come (and were already slowly taking off by the time the Medici gained power) were in place: the city was thriving economically, thanks to the wise rule of its new leaders, and its society was stable and dynamic.

Rediscovery of the Ancient Past

As Florence and the rest of Northern Italy emerged as the new economic and social center of Western Europe, the situation was ripe for a massive cultural breakthrough, which manifested when the Italians started to place more and more emphasis on the rediscovery and celebration of classical texts. This process also started around the 14th century, and by the time the Medici took over Florence, it was at its peak.

One of the most influential of those who jump-started the cultural achievements of the Renaissance is Francisco Petrarca, better known as Petrarch. A poet and scholar of Tuscan descent, Petrarch received his education in the southern French town of Avignon during the first half of the 14th century. During this time, conflicts and rivalries in the papacy and the influence of the French kings had resulted in the turbulent "Avignon Papacy" period, when two rival popes simultaneously claimed to be the head of the Catholic Church. One of them had a court in Avignon, which meant that the French town had a concentration of well-educated clergymen and lawyers. Petrarch was thus lucky to end up in Avignon, where he became a master of the ancient Latin language and started copying ancient works from manuscripts available in the papal court there. At this time, essentially the only people who had access to these texts were the clergy, but few were as enthusiastic about uncovering more of them as Petrarch. His passion for learning eventually led to the recovery of the great Roman writer Cicero's *Letters to Athens* from the cathedral of Verona, further motivating the Tuscan youngster to continue searching for ancient manuscripts. He traveled throughout Europe and found more and more such texts, which had been stored deep within the libraries and crypts of the old Christian cathedrals. Ultimately, Petrarch became one of the most prominent scholars of 14th-century Europe, accruing great knowledge of ancient literature and spreading his passion to many others, like Giovani Boccaccio, who also started to collect classical literature.

Petrarch, Boccaccio, and other collectors and scholars of the classical texts found something new, something compelling, about these texts. Unlike the scholastic tradition of the medieval world, which focused primarily on the study of law, medicine, and theology through the application of reason to philosophical and theological questions, these texts shifted attention to the study of liberal arts that were perceived to be of great importance during antiquity. Logic, grammar, music, astronomy, geometry, arithmetic, rhetoric, and metaphysics were all subjects adhered to by ancient Romans. Together, they made up the *humanitas* (humanities)—a category that emphasized wisdom and virtue, the exploration of which gave more intellectual freedom and satisfaction to the individual. Thus, those who studied the humanities were dubbed humanists, and the movement they began was known as humanism.

A crucial development in the mid-15th century in the East accelerated the development of humanism and the spread of a passion for learning. In 1453, the Ottoman Turks laid siege and captured the great city of Constantinople. The Byzantine Empire, which had survived for about a thousand years after the fall of Rome, was destroyed. Muslim Turks had pressured the Byzantines for many decades, and the territories of the once-great Eastern Roman Empire were slowly taken over. The fall of Constantinople and the preceding events that led to it resulted in the migration of Byzantine Greek scholars to the West, and most of them ended up in Italy. They brought with them even more classical texts and culture of ancient Greece, which had been relatively well-preserved but unavailable to the rest of Europe due to the socio-political and cultural division between the Byzantines and the West. Ideas brought by Byzantium were translated from ancient Greek into Latin and other modern languages and diffused greatly with the existing learning tradition that had begun in the early 14th century. Most importantly, the rediscovery of classical Greek philosophy, mythology, and history was vital to the development of the humanist movement and eventually emerged as one of the staples of the Renaissance.

Therefore, as more and more of the classical past was uncovered in the 14th–15th centuries, the medieval way of thought that had remained stagnant for several hundred years began to evolve. Humanism viewed the classical past as the most glorious era in history and celebrated the intellectual achievements and moral virtues of ancient Romans and Greeks. They believed that the medieval scholastic tradition had focused on trivial things while ignoring something far more important—the nature of man. This central aspect of humanist thought was greatly influenced by Greek philosophers like Aristotle and Plato, who had posed questions regarding morality, virtues, and truth and wanted to learn more about these phenomena outside the traditional lens of understanding. Withdrawing into philosophy and just speculation was not enough for the humanists. They needed to posit the ideals of man so that everyone could attain them. Early Renaissance thought bridged the gap to classical antiquity, which had put humans, with all their best and worst qualities, at the center of their universe and sought to revive this understanding and institutionalize it in the minds of medieval people.

Chapter Three – The Essence of the Renaissance

Drive to Synthesize

The main outcome of the rediscovery of and better familiarization with classical antiquity was the drive to understand more by synthesizing classicism and Christianity. Old texts emphasized the ability of humans to basically achieve anything they wanted. Petrarch was one of the first to reassert that. He believed in the innate ability of humanity to be wise and make conscious, rational decisions, and this did not exactly mean the abandonment of the Christian way of life. Humanist thought was unique because it sought to combine the main morality of Christianity with the best version of man that was to be found in classical antiquity.

For example, one area where this manifested perfectly was the re-adoption of a certain outlook on life strongly celebrated in ancient Rome and Greece: individual involvement in public affairs. Ancient Romans and Greeks hailed the principles of republicanism and democracy. They believed that a truly wise and kind man must get involved in the most pressing issues of his city or state. If one could in any way contribute to bettering public life, be it through teaching, taking up arms, or voting, it was almost expected. For the ancient thinkers, a strong state was complementary to the formation of a thriving, self-sustaining, virtuous society, and vice-versa. The branch of humanism that re-emphasized this is often referred to as civic humanism. Civic humanists believed ancient Greek and Roman societies were so prosperous because people understood how important it was to be involved in public affairs for the greater good. Those who failed to do so were undeserving of being considered "good."

Early Renaissance retained its close ties with Christianity. This was not unexpected since, by that time, the Christian way of life had become a normality for Europe. Instead, it synthesized the best of classicism and Christianity, and the way it did this was marvelous. The most prominent example is Dante's *Divine Comedy*, written in 1321. In his masterpiece, Dante voyages through Hell, Purgatory, and Heaven (all of which were part of Christian doctrine and depicted so). There, Dante encounters historical and mythological beings, some awaiting their entry to Heaven and some suffering terribly for their sins. Among those suffering are people from contemporary Italy known to be corrupt, fraudulent, or evil. Dante thus employed civic humanism in this way, too—he painted the failure to participate in public processes for the greater good and deliberate malicious actions as among the worst sins through a Christian lens. This was a rather creative example of how classical tradition was combined with the Christian outlook on life. *Divine Comedy* remains one of the best works of literature to this day.

Another way the synthesis of Christian and classical understandings of life was achieved was by reinterpreting classical antiquity through a Christian lens. The work of classical poets, such as Virgil—a central character in Dante's *Divine Comedy* whose epic *Aeneid* sought to personify the ideals of a virtuous Roman citizen—were reinterpreted. The main character of the epic, Aeneas, was depicted by humanists as allegorically undergoing a Christian struggle to find salvation and purity of soul through his journey of seeking duty for the great Roman Empire, as mentioned in the original epic. This was a way of appropriating the classical ideology and outlook on life in contemporary settings. Humanists claimed that classical tradition was not incompatible with what Christianity stood for and sought to amplify the relationship between the two.

In fact, not only did the Renaissance not abandon Christianity for antiquity, it was likely the period when Europe embraced the religion the most. Hundreds of new cathedrals and churches were constructed in Italy and throughout the continent, which had distinctive Renaissance architectural styles and were decorated with works of Renaissance artists. Religious education also took off, and more and more people started to indulge themselves in the study of Christian scriptures and doctrines.

This resulted in the further institutionalization of Catholicism in the lives of every European. Additionally, with more time devoted to the study of doctrine and the essence of the religion, the late Renaissance gave birth to one of the most influential religious diversities to emerge from Christianity: the Protestant Reformation. Later, we will cover how Protestantism was born in 16th-century Germany and built on the humanist ideas proposed in the early Renaissance to transform the lives of millions of Christians forever.

The Individual Back in Center

A fundamental break of the Renaissance from the way of thought of the early Middle Ages was putting humans back at the center of attention. During the Renaissance, men and women were reasonable beings, capable of attaining wisdom, morality, and virtue by themselves without the guidance of the Christian Church that had been imposed on Europeans increasingly after the fall of Rome. Just as in classical antiquity, individuals could be great and heroic. They could venture out to the unknown with the desire to learn more about the world and themselves and emerge successful in their endeavors. They were no longer to be considered eternally stained by original sin. Rather, they could and would prosper in a world full of possibilities if they tried hard enough and put their all into it. Independence and autonomy of choice were emphasized by humanism and considered to be the greatest qualities humans possessed. The emphasis on individualism also resulted, in a way, in the development of the autobiography as a common genre of literature. More and more people undertook writing diaries, for example, which only further boosted the desire to learn.

The definition of what it meant to be civilized was also expanded. At first, the Italian high society began to dress better and cleaner and behave more proudly. Good manners and general conduct were appreciated, and more and more writers emphasized this. Castiglione, for example, stressed the need to institutionalize higher conduct. People should understand why they were behaving the way they were and then effortlessly act that way, with their behavior becoming an essential, natural part of them, like breathing. This was largely based on breakthroughs in humanist thought of what it meant to be virtuous, polite, and wise, and more attention was devoted to stoic manners. People started to speculate what it meant to be an "ideal man," once again combining what they had rediscovered in classical tradition with what their Christian life had taught them. Knowing how to read and write in several languages, familiarity with public etiquette that was becoming increasingly dynamic, being capable of painting, singing, playing musical instruments, or being good at physical activities generally came to be valued more. Education and a will to learn and explore were also vital for the idealistic vision of the "Renaissance man," even if they were rather unattainable for most people, who had no means to pursue so many passions at once.

On the other hand, the Renaissance's claim of having rediscovered the essence of humanity meant little progress regarding the status of women, who continued to live under the same social restrictions as before. This was partly because women were still considered the sinful descendants of biblical Eve. For this reason, they were associated mostly with negative emotions and attributes such as deceit, chaos, and jealousy. They were often depicted this way in Renaissance art (something we will touch on later). In families, boys were almost always favored over girls, who were either quickly married off or sent to convents, where at least they could get some education. Women were regarded as less competent in almost all activities, a conception that would persist for many more centuries.

Chapter Four – Italian Renaissance Art

Proto-Renaissance

Renaissance art is what the period is perhaps most remembered for. In Italy, Leonardo da Vinci, Raphael, Michelangelo, Titian, Sandro Botticelli, Donatello, and others pioneered breakthroughs in painting and sculpture; German and Dutch artists such as Albrecht Durer, Jan Van Eyck, and Rogier van der Weyden further explored the artistic horizons. Like every other aspect of the period, Renaissance art manifested the new way of thought introduced with the onset of humanism and the rediscovery of classical traditions. Evolving from religious scenery and themes, which dominated painting before the Renaissance, Renaissance paintings also placed humans at the center of attention, outlining their physicality and seeking to explore their inner emotions. Renaissance painters depicted everything from ancient mythology to historical events, biblical pieces, and everyday life. Through the development of new painting techniques and a more complete understanding of the human body, Renaissance painters produced some of the most memorable pieces of art to this day. Similar things can be said about sculpture and architecture, which improved massively, borrowing heavily from ancient times.

Before we examine the essence of Renaissance art and how it developed over a century and a half, it is first better to look at how what came directly before the Renaissance revolutionized the human understanding of art. By the 13th century, as already mentioned, religious themes dominated painting. In Italy, artists often based their works on Byzantine (Greek) iconography, developing the Italo-Byzantine style. Painted on small, portable canvases and utilizing the tempera medium derived from mixing water-soluble pigments with egg yolk (whose main advantage was that it dried fast), these paintings all looked rather similar. For example, although commissioned by different churches or cathedrals, depictions of the Madonna and Child were usually done on a golden background, and the details of the characters inside the paintings were often fixed or hardly modified. Taking center stage, the Virgin would hold Jesus in one position, with her head tilted the same way, wearing similar clothes and with similar, subtle facial expressions. This was the universally accepted way to depict the Madonna and Child, and the pioneers of medieval art, such as the Florentine Cimabue and Sienese Duccio, always painted them this way.

By the end of the 13th century, a new painter burst onto the artistic scene of Northern Italy, one who is often considered the influence from which other Renaissance artists borrowed significantly. Giotto di Bondone, better known as simply Giotto, was an apprentice of Cimabue who made one of the first breakthroughs in medieval Italo-Byzantine painting. His style was distinct from his predecessors in that he depicted more dynamic scenes and made the figures of the characters fully three-dimensional. Giotto was one of the first whose paintings told some sort of a story and had characters dynamically interacting with one another. His style was an evolution of the iconographic style of the Byzantine school, with his characters having distinct characteristics in different paintings and frescoes he completed. *The Lamentation* is probably the most celebrated of Giotto's works. Biblical characters lamenting Christ and the angels depicted above all have distinctive facial features and emotions. They are in motion and are fully interacting with each other. This was vastly different from the works of his predecessors, who essentially repeated the attributes of their characters and depicted them as ascetic, detached beings.

Giotto, Lamentation (The Mourning of Christ)
https://commons.wikimedia.org/wiki/File:Compianto_sul_Cristo_morto.jpg

Early Renaissance Art

Historians consider the year 1425 as the end of the Proto-Renaissance period and the beginning of the Early Renaissance, which was once again mostly concentrated in Florence and immediately surrounding areas. By this time, Giotto had already become a renowned artist in Northern Italy, and his contemporaries were starting to emulate his style, which was unknowingly revolutionizing art as they knew it. They stuck to depicting biblical scenes, of course, and were mainly employed by different churches to complete their interior design with frescoes. For example, *Annunciation of the Shepherds* stands out in the Florentine Church of Santa Croce. Painted by Taddeo Gaddi, the figures inside the fresco are all clearly in motion and interacting with one another. They have distinct three-dimensional shapes, much like those in Giotto's work. What's special about *Annunciation* is the color contrast, as the bright upper half of the fresco greatly contrasts with the darker lower half, making it one of the earliest works that utilized shading in such detail.

Unfortunately, the misfortunes brought by the Black Death in the latter half of the 14th century halted the developments of the Renaissance a bit, or at least postponed them to the beginning of the 15th century. Around the same time, the public perception of artists began to change. Before, they were mostly considered craftsmen—people one could simply hire to do the job one wanted, just as one could have hired an artisan or a potter for their services. But a change of attitude towards art coincided with the breakthroughs of humanism and the gradual rediscovery of ancient works, which emphasized the beauty of the soul and celebrated human ability, viewing art as something prestigious, not just another profession. Artists no longer regarded painting or sculpting as something they did because they needed the money to survive.

Leonardo da Vinci, perhaps the man who most represents the spirit of the Renaissance, considered his work a manifestation of "higher art," not a mere profession or craft. Humanist ideology, which emphasized learning and the pursuit of greatness and perfection, played a big role in developing such an understanding. Artists started to believe that they should constantly improve their work, even if it took years. Motivated to perfectly capture the essence of this or that biblical, mythological, or historical event, they thus started to increasingly journey beyond the bounds of traditional art styles, focusing on trying to make the viewer understand the severity and seriousness of the situations depicted in their paintings. Soon, a byproduct of this was that paintings started to feel more real and natural as characters became more dynamic and started to resemble real human beings with real feelings.

The Neoplatonist understanding of life, rediscovered with humanism and developed as a rather prominent outlook, also contributed to this conception of art. Neoplatonism suggested that ideas such as goodness or beauty existed outside the realm perceivable to humans in everyday life. It emphasized the need to perfect oneself to attain the closest possible version of these ideals. This conception was increasingly shared by Renaissance artists as the movement matured. Throughout the development of Renaissance art, one can observe how, from monotonous paintings that depict characters that are identical in their forms and manners, paintings began to become more diversified. This evolution can be observed in the works of one the first truly Renaissance artists—Massaccio—whose fresco, *The Tribute Money,* is still in the

Brancacci Chapel of the Basilica de Santa Maria del Carmine in Florence. The fresco depicts a biblical scene in which Jesus instructs Peter to find a coin in a fish's mouth to pay the temple tax. Jesus is pictured with his disciples and one tax collector in the center. The fresco can be further divided into two additional parts to the left and right sides. On the left, we can see Peter by the water, searching for the coin, while on the right, he can be observed already paying the tax collector.

The Tribute Money *by Masaccio*
https://commons.wikimedia.org/wiki/File:Masaccio7.jpg

This is a bit strange at first—how exactly does the fresco attempt to tell the whole biblical scene at once, and why is Peter depicted three times at three different points inside the fresco? This is exactly what is revolutionary with Masaccio's work. This was a fresco unlike anything of its time, combining three different parts of the biblical scene with a trick. In the fresco, Christ is what's known as the vanishing point, a point inside the painting toward which eyes are drawn first. The clever use of single-point perspective and color contrast amplifies the visual effect of the fresco. Additional scenes are only then noticed, creating a cohesive picture. Overall, the painting is dynamic, achieved partly by using new techniques. On the other hand, the new objective to depict beauty realistically—something emphasized greatly by humanism—is also present, making the fresco a stylistically distinct piece of work.

Crucially, the early 15th century also saw a massive increase in artists' guilds. New, aspiring artists would enroll in these organizations as apprentices of more senior painters and sculptors and undergo formal training. As time passed, the status of these guilds increased, and the quality of their painting rose, as well. By the mid-15th century, prestigious guilds competed, and guilds of different cities developed their own distinctive styles, or schools, of painting. Eventually, the Venetian school, for example, which included distinguished Renaissance painters such as Titian, Giorgione, Veronese, and Tintoretto, emphasized the subtlety of colors and their effortless diffusion with each other over the use of clear lines to differentiate between the subjects of the paintings. Successful "graduates" of artists' guilds were recognized by contemporaries and employed for the rest of their lives, hired by private citizens who wished to decorate their estates and enrich their collections or different churches.

In Italy, the development of a tradition of patronage of the arts was just as important as the development of new techniques and styles in the arts for the flourishing of the Renaissance. For example, wealthy families, some of old patrician descent and some having obtained their riches thanks to the recent economic growth, would cordially invite distinguished painters to their rich villas and commission them with work. This was also beneficial for painters, who could work for their patrons without restrictions or distractions and deliver the best quality work they could—which went in tandem with their new humanist outlook on life.

Humanist scholars were also fortunate enough to receive patronage from the wealthy as their or their children's educators. Having obtained general knowledge of the humanities and natural sciences, they made great tutors. They were good secretaries and advisors, paying close attention to improving the behavior of their patrons, developing the official conduct inside their courts, and taking charge of correspondence with other individuals of status. This was largely because the renewed interest in an active life also included paying attention to things that might have seemed trivial to Europe of the Middle Ages. How one was involved in public affairs was just as important as *what* was done, and the whole procedure should exert wisdom and a sense of familiarization with the new norms. Wealthy families should not behave well just because they were wealthy. Rather, they should institutionalize good conduct and manners, making them a part of everyday life—an endeavor in which the tutors came in extremely handy.

The Medici were among the most prominent patrons of the arts. Thanks to their excessive wealth, they often commissioned architects to design their estates, for example. In turn, such close contact with the vanguard of cultural development elevated the status of the Medici and made them far more prestigious than they already were. Cosimo de'

Medici, for example, the man responsible for growing the influence of his family, was a passionate collector of ancient manuscripts and devoted time from his busy schedule to learning. The Medici financed the often-ambitious projects envisioned by Renaissance artists, who needed a lot of materials and time to complete their work. Knowing they were set in all other ways, artists thus put their hearts and souls into pursuing their passion and producing the best they could. Michelangelo, for example, was one of the most prominent of those who benefitted from the goodwill of the Medici, even getting to design the Medici tomb in the Basilica of Saint Lawrence in Florence. The humanist education of the patrons also resulted in them often specifying what they wanted the artists to do—which scenes or characters to depict and how. Personal portraits or everyday themes were also common. The artist and the commissioner agreed on the price, first based on the order size, for example, and later on an assessment of the artist's skill.

An interesting practice that became common when artist-patron relations changed for the better, for example, was including the patron inside the painting as one of the characters. Like most other things in Renaissance art, this was much different from what came before. Masaccio's *The Adoration of the Magi,* one of the most celebrated works of the early Renaissance painted in 1426, features the portraits of the notary who commissioned the painting and his son. In this way, artists often paid homage to those who "looked after" them, growing the bonds between them and their patrons even more and developing a more cohesive, friendly, and dynamic culture where cooperation was just as valued as skill.

Interestingly, however, it is not a painting that is considered the earliest Renaissance work in Florence. It is, rather, a church door for the Florence Baptistery, designed by Lorenzo Ghiberti for a competition held to specifically select the best design in 1401. Based on the biblical theme of the Sacrifice of Isaac, Ghiberti's work features a small relief sculpture on the surface of the door, depicting the scene. Its style is reminiscent of the other paintings we mentioned earlier. Characters are dynamic and alive, with distinct characteristics, and all come together to create a scene. The work is heavily influenced by classical art, as, for example, Isaac is depicted as a masculine man with a great physique—a prominent characteristic of ancient Greek and Roman art pieces since a healthy body was believed to have a healthy soul. The Florence Baptistery features sets of doors designed by artists other than Ghiberti, who took twenty-seven years to complete his work after winning the competition.

The Sacrifice of Isaac
MenkinAlRire, CC BY-SA 4.0 <https://creativecommons.org/licenses/by-sa/4.0>, via Wikimedia Commons; https://de.wikipedia.org/wiki/Datei:Lorenzo_Ghiberti,_The_Sacrifice_of_Isaac,1401-2,_Florence,_Bargello.jpg#file

In short, the first half of the 15th century was crucial for developing the artistic culture in Northern Italy. Thanks to stylistic and technological breakthroughs in painting and sculpture and the strong patronage of the arts by the wealthy families of Florence, Venice, Milan, and other cities, early 15th-century artists were essentially the vanguard of the great things that would come after them. Thanks to the development of new techniques that uniquely captured and utilized light, paid more attention to shadows and perspective, and depicted characters as dynamic beings with emotions and distinct physical attributes that interacted with each other, art became very different from what it had been for the previous few hundred years. Artists like Masaccio and Masolino became great inspirations for the gigantic figures of the High Renaissance—the period that came after the first half of the 15th century.

High Renaissance

In arts, the period known as the High Renaissance started at the end of the 15th century, around 1490. Lasting until about 1530 in Italy, this era's works are perhaps the most recognizable of all art. Of course, as in most events throughout history, the break from the Early Renaissance did not happen at once, so no point can be identified as the beginning of the High Renaissance. What contributed to the development of the style of the period was the shift of the patronage role from the wealthy to the Catholic Church. Indeed, by the end of the century, Italy was struck with a subtle economic recession, the effects of which would only magnify as years passed. This was because of the complex political climate that existed in the region. When the city-states were at the height of their political and economic power, bigger nations became increasingly interested in gobbling them up. France and the Holy Roman Empire showed increasing interest in expanding their territories and influencing the prosperous city-states of Northern Italy like Florence, Genoa, and Milan. Spain, on the other hand, mostly focused its attention on the southern part of the peninsula. These external factors further contributed to the escalation of already-turbulent relations the highest classes of these cities had with each other, resulting in increased struggles for power and influence. This turmoil had a ripple effect on Renaissance art, which until then comfortably enjoyed the patronage of the wealthy families of Northern Europe.

Luckily, however, artists of that time found refuge in another equally (or arguably even more) reputable patron—the Church. Of course, patrician families still employed various artists to work on their estates, but the upper hand was assumed by the papacy, which had grown its power and influence exponentially. Indeed, as already mentioned, with the importance of Catholicism growing throughout Europe amid the political troubles in the East and in Iberia, the Church had become one of the main arbiters of affairs in Europe. The papacy had also accrued enough means to start rebuilding the ruined territories of central Italy it controlled, including the once-great city of Rome, which had been reduced to a shadow of its former self due to constant invasions throughout the Middle Ages. In the 1470s, excavation projects had uncovered much of ancient Rome, parts of the city that had been completely forgotten. This was partly due to the renewed interest in classical antiquity, which owed a lot to the development of humanist thought. The wealth of the Church was also constantly increasing, as opposed to private families, who were dependent on the existing social dynamics.

Thus, the time was right for the Church to once again take the lead in financing and looking after the artists. By this time, however, art had moved on from the relatively universal and monotonous Italo-Byzantine style and had become far more expressive than ever. The development of new techniques and the increasing interest in more realistic and creative depictions was an opportunity for the Church. The Church claimed it was the most influential and oldest institution in Europe, embodying stability, peace, and the spirit of human life through its God-given mandate. Visual aesthetics were important in reinforcing this image, and employing some of the brightest artistic minds to design the interiors and exteriors of churches, religious courts, and papal palaces was a great way to achieve this.

Art of the High Renaissance was greatly influenced by this sense of aggrandizement under the papacy's influence. Therefore, it is no surprise that art became far larger than before. High Renaissance artists painted on huge canvases, and their paintings would often be the only thing hanging up on the huge halls of papal residences. This is not to speak of the frescoes and sculptures from this period, which would often take multiple years to complete. The content of the art and the style also became quite complex, as if evolving from the works of the Early Renaissance period. The High Renaissance realized the increasing diversion of artists from the depiction of rational order to grand, ambitious scenery aimed at obtaining a powerful reaction from the audience. Canvases were filled with complicated scenes that were aesthetically pleasing due to the impressive way the characters were depicted. Michelangelo's work in the Vatican's Sistine Chapel is one example. Michelangelo glorified the physical and emotional attributes of his biblical, mythological, and historical characters, sometimes to the point that the many details in the frescoes overwhelm the viewers. Paying great attention to detail and the perfection of techniques, High Renaissance art can indeed be considered the magnum opus of Renaissance art or art in general. The distinct style to which it gave birth is called Mannerism (Grand Manner), capturing the essence of art from this period. The heightened scale, dramatic, exaggerated imagery, complexity, and attention to detail are all attributes of Mannerism that dominated the High Renaissance.

During the High Renaissance, some of the most iconic names in the history of art emerged. Leonardo da Vinci, Raphael, and Michelangelo are often considered the "big three" in this period of rebirth, though artists like Titian, Giorgione, and Bellini are also among some of the most memorable names from this period. In this chapter, we will look at these artists and examine what makes them so special in the context of the Renaissance and art in general.

Leonardo da Vinci - The Renaissance Man

If one person will forever be associated with the Renaissance and everything it stood for, it is certainly Leonardo da Vinci. Da Vinci was born in 1452 in Florence, and his father was a distinguished notary in the city. Through him, young Leonardo ended up in the workshop of Andre del Verrocchio, where he greatly developed his artistic capabilities in painting and sculpture. Having a creative mind from a young age, da Vinci was interested in studying more about the world around him. His personal notebooks from his formative years depict many sketches of different things, such as military weapons or mechanisms of various uses. In the 1470s, Leonardo was accepted into Florence's guild of artists, but it was around 1482 that he truly began his successful career. In early 1482, at the invitation of Duke Ludovico Sforza of Milan, the 30-year-old Leonardo decided to pursue his career prospects in Milan, being employed in the duke's court. It is unknown exactly what attracted the artist to Sforza's court, especially since he had just landed some of the biggest commissions of his early career as a member of the Florentine guild. However, he abandoned the projects he had started to work on in his native city and remained in Milan for the next seventeen years before eventually returning to Florence in the year 1500.

Even though da Vinci is often remembered first and foremost as a painter, his body of work is relatively small, and only seventeen of his paintings survive. What characterizes his style the most are two aspects. The first is his ability to capture human emotion. Art experts often praise Leonardo for expressing a wide range of emotions with the faces of his characters. His *Mona Lisa*, of course, is a prime example of this. Completed during the final years of his life, the *Mona Lisa* revolutionized how portraits were to be painted. The half-body of the only character of the painting—arguably the wife of Florentine merchant Francesco del Giocondo—is the main focus. She is sitting down with a deep, subtle, infamous smile, in great harmony with her ambiguous background of nature. The two parts of the painting effortlessly fuse with each other, perhaps symbolizing the overall link of human beauty and nature and the fact that the two coexist and should coexist at all times. Effortless fusion and transition between objects of interest are achieved thanks to a technique that Leonardo pioneered himself—sfumato or "shadow." This is the second most prominent characteristic of Leonardo's paintings. The subtle brush strokes produce an effect of the manipulation of shade and color, thus leading to a seamless transition from light to dark colors without using sharp lines to contrast objects from one another. Sfumato is what makes Leonardo's paintings truly unique. The tones it generates help the viewer seamlessly move their eyes from one point of the painting to another and amplify the mysteriousness and the range of emotions captured on the faces of da Vinci's paintings, as in the *Mona Lisa*.

The Mona Lisa by Leonardo da Vinci
https://commons.wikimedia.org/wiki/File:Mona_Lisa,_by_Leonardo_da_Vinci,_from_C2RMF_r etouched.jpg

Another of Leonardo's iconic paintings is the *Last Supper*. Painted in the mid-1490s in Milan's Santa Maria delle Grazie, it depicts the exact moment in the Bible when Jesus tells his apostles that one of them will betray him. Shocked by this news, the apostles are depicted to be agitated, discussing among themselves with great animation. Jesus sits in the center, in splendid isolation from the rest of the chaos. The only other character in the painting that is depicted as calm as Jesus is Judas, who, sitting to the right of Jesus and wearing green, realizes his mistake and has a deep look on his face, contemplating his decision to betray Jesus. The composition narrates the biblical scene, greatly capturing the confusion and chaos that emerges at the Last Supper after Jesus reveals that he knows of his betrayal. All the characters have distinguishable expressions and seamlessly interact with each other, creating a great scene overall that flows smoothly. Unfortunately, partly due to Leonardo's indecisiveness regarding what technique to use to paint the fresco, the painting deteriorated by the mid-16th century and was not restored until after World War II. Still, Leonardo's *Last Supper* became a footprint for all future depictions of this scene and is still celebrated today for its innovativeness and ability to narrate the story.

The Last Supper by Leonardo da Vinci
https://commons.wikimedia.org/wiki/File:%C3%9Altima_Cena_-_Da_Vinci_5.jpg

As much as he was a painter, however, Leonardo was also a scientist, biologist, anatomist, botanist, architect, sculptor, physicist, and engineer. Due to his undying curiosity, he personally researched all these fields, mastering his understanding of natural and physical sciences only to use this knowledge in his artistic career. Leonardo deeply believed that first-hand experience and knowledge of the human body, for example, was conducive to good painting. He also believed it was a good painter's obligation to make their characters as realistic as possible by employing the knowledge of anatomy. This was a very humanist conception of human ability—Leonardo thought that humans could perfect their work by putting in enough effort to study the subjects they wished to paint, the trajectory of light and shadows, and the nature of perspective. In his notebooks, which he carried with him all the time, he made annotations in pencil, observing the objects around him and pondering how they operated in real life to best capture them in painting or sculpture. In addition to including well-known concepts, Leonardo also explained relatively new ideas about spatial organization in paintings through lighting and shadows and concepts such as lateral recession, all of which would be expanded by his successors. One thing about his notetaking that is rather unusual and further emphasizes his genius is his ability to mirror-write. Since he was left-handed and extremely talented, mirror writing probably came naturally to him, and his sketches and notes can only be deciphered if one reads them with a mirror.

There are hints in Leonardo's writings that he was probably compiling his knowledge to produce a comprehensive, proto-scientific study of painting. By combining his vast theoretical framework with practical applications of the knowledge he had gathered, his book or treatise could have been directed toward aspiring artists as a potential guide to painting. In it, various techniques and their applications would be explained, and his main idea would be to promote the *saper vedere*—the art of knowing how to see. He deemed this very important, especially for anyone who claimed to be an artist. From his notebooks, we can see that Leonardo considered painting and sculpture not just another profession but a higher form of work, a humanitarian subject or a science of its own. In the long term, his emphasis on implementing empirical evidence and experimentation may have influenced the development of the scientific method, which transformed the way scientific studies are conducted in all fields.

Leonardo da Vinci is also the man who almost single-handedly accelerated the study of anatomy. Again, anatomy and the understanding of the human body was something he hoped to use in his artistic work, in his pursuit of perfecting his style and technique. Probably interested in the subject from his days with his teacher, Verrocchio, he invested more time into his research once he moved to Milan. Working with several prominent hospitals of the time, Leonardo was permitted to dissect human bodies to better comprehend their fundamental structure. Primarily, he was concerned with studying parts closely linked with motion, such as the skeletal structure and muscles. Mechanical activity was of great interest because he would most often be painting it, and the knowledge seemed most useful to him. We can see his deep understanding of the human physique from his sketches, which are dotted with graphic depictions of the body in different positions, both static and in motion. Though he was technically not a professional doctor or anatomist, he nevertheless helped advance the contemporary understanding of the subject and demonstrated his skill in art. His *Vitruvian Man*, which also takes its place as one of the most instantly recognizable paintings, is a great demonstration of the knowledge he gathered of the human body and the application of geometrical principles to it—another field he greatly loved. The perfection of the *Vitruvian Man* reflects the existing humanist outlook on life: the human body with all its perfections and imperfections could be considered a microcosm, a symbol for the greater universe. Understanding it was just the first step in understanding the much larger world.

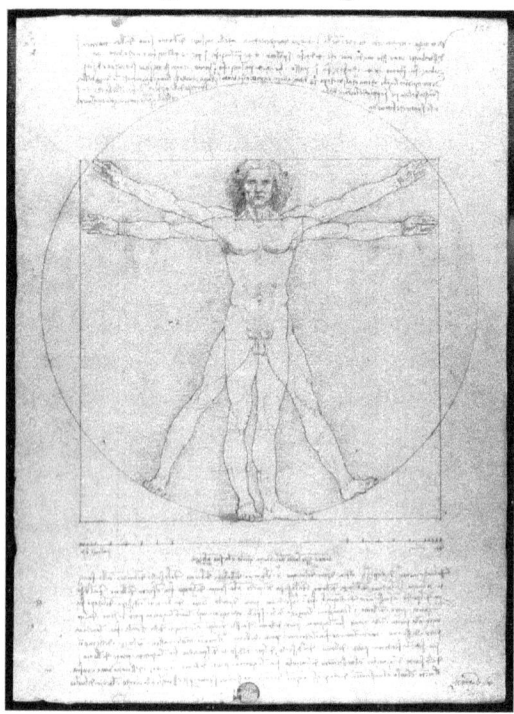

Vitruvian Man by Leonardo da Vinci
https://en.wikipedia.org/wiki/File:Da_Vinci_Vitruve_Luc_Viatour.jpg

Last but not least, Leonardo can be considered a brilliant engineer and an architect. Having a creative eye and a deep understanding of key mathematical, physics, and geometric principles, it is unsurprising that Leonardo's notebooks are full of interesting designs, ranging from military to civilian technology, public and private buildings, and plans for whole towns. Through diagrams and patterns, he identified different machines and the mechanics behind them, such as transmission gears or hydraulic presses. Leonardo helped his cities greatly with his practical knowledge, helping design canals, fortifications, streets, and overall urban planning. He also developed the first prototypes of the modern tank and flying machines, rather carefully outlining the physics behind them but ultimately lacking a power source to generate enough for his works to come to fruition.

All in all, Leonardo da Vinci, with his undying will for self-improvement and exploration of the world, and his application of the knowledge gathered from empirical experience to the arts to perfect his work, is the person who most embodies the spirit of the Renaissance. A man of many talents and interests, he not only revolutionized painting and produced the most iconic artistic works to this day but also significantly expanded knowledge in most fields of science. Leonardo refreshed the Renaissance with his ambitious projects and big ideas. He was already considered among the most accomplished people in Italy when he passed away in 1519.

Michelangelo and the Grandeur of the Renaissance

After Leonardo da Vinci, the artist who comes to the minds of many who explore the Renaissance is Michelangelo di Lodovico Buonarroti Simoni, better known by his first name. A younger contemporary of Leonardo, Michelangelo was born in 1475 to an aristocratic family in Florence and became one of the most renowned artists in history throughout his almost 90 years of life. Much like Leonardo, he did not only limit himself to painting and pursued sculpture and architecture very enthusiastically. In fact, despite his monumental achievements in these three fields, he considered himself primarily a sculptor, as he never abandoned the practice throughout his career, focusing on painting and architectural design only in certain periods of his life. Considered the most talented artist of his time, Michelangelo is an example of a Renaissance artist who became extremely popular during his lifetime, with his biography published by his contemporary, Giorgio Vasari, in 1550. To this day, he remains one of the most influential artists ever, the author of some of the most iconic works that still inspire and amaze millions today and embody the essence of the High Renaissance the most clearly.

Much like Leonardo, Michelangelo also started out as an apprentice of an accomplished painter, Domenico Ghirlandaio, during his teens. He was quickly recognized by Lorenzo de Medici, through whom he became more acquainted with classical antiquity—one of his main sources of inspiration throughout his career. It was through Medici and the sculptors associated with the ruler of Florence that he got into sculpting. However, he preferred to work in marble rather than bronze, which was more common in his day. This was undoubtedly due to the influence of classical antiquity on the young artist. By the end of the 15th century, due to the decline that had beset Florence and the Medici family, Michelangelo moved to Bologna and then to Rome, completing the first of his major projects—the tomb of St. Dominic. The influences and the developing style of Michelangelo can clearly be seen in the design and the grandness of the tomb, which would become definitive features of most of the artist's work. The statue of *Bacchus*, completed in 1497, is the earliest surviving large statue by Michelangelo. Forging the ancient Greek god of wine from one large life-sized marble block, Michelangelo created a statue that effectively captures the essence of Bacchus as he is depicted in Greek mythology. He is a youthful, lively god who cares a lot about entertainment and drinking, but his deep, focused gaze on the winecup he is holding hints at the fact that he has become a victim of his own self. *Bacchus* is one of the first examples of Michelangelo's work where his deep technical understanding of marble sculpting, human physique, and emotion combined with his knowledge of the ancient world.

Bacchus by Michelangelo
https://commons.wikimedia.org/wiki/File:Michelangelo_Bacchus.jpg

This work served as a great introduction to Michelangelo's career. Two years later, he completed his *Pieta*, which has become an iconic work of the artist. Commissioned by a French cardinal, *Pieta* portrays the Virgin holding Jesus after the Crucifixion. Lamenting her son on her knees, the relationship between the two bodies is seamless, giving it a pyramid structure. Mary is depicted as a younger version of herself as described in the Bible and looks down on Jesus, whose lifeless, skinny body is resting on her overwhelmingly large gown. Michelangelo again sculpted both figures from one marble block, which was very difficult. *Pieta* is hailed as one of the finest works of the Renaissance, as it captures the contrast between life and death, man and woman, horizontal and vertical, while at the same time marvelously outlining the physical and emotional attributes of the characters.

The Pieta by Michelangelo

Michelangelo, CC BY-SA 3.0 <http://creativecommons.org/licenses/by-sa/3.0/>, via Wikimedia Commons; https://commons.wikimedia.org/wiki/File:Michelangelo%27s_Pieta_5450_cropncleaned.jpg

After *Pieta* came perhaps the most renowned work of Michelangelo—an expression that is up to interpretation since all his works are so renowned. *David*, which was commissioned to the artist in 1501, was unveiled at the central square in front of the Palazzo della Signoria in Florence in 1504. Coming in at 5.17 meters (17 feet) tall, *David* can be considered Michelangelo's first true homage to classical antiquity, reflected in giving the statue such a large size, characteristic of classical sculptures. To this day, *David* is considered among the best examples of what the Renaissance (and the humanist movement, in general) stood for—the excellence and perfection of the human body and, thus, according to the contemporary perception, of the human soul. With *David*, Michelangelo demonstrated that his understanding of the human body had only increased after his debut. Initially, since the authorities of the Florence Cathedral had commissioned the artist to complete the statue, they had considered placing it on the cathedral's rooftop. As Michelangelo neared completion, however, it became apparent that the statue was too big to be lifted to the top, and instead, a council convened to decide where it would be put. Many artists and city authorities were present, including Leonardo da Vinci and Sandro Botticelli.

David by Michelangelo

Michelangelo, CC BY-SA 4.0 <https://creativecommons.org/licenses/by-sa/4.0>, via Wikimedia Commons; https://commons.wikimedia.org/wiki/File:Michelangelo%27s_David_-_right_view_2.jpg

David and other works from the early 1500s, including the statue *Madonna of Bruges* and the painting *The Holy Family*, contributed greatly to the development of Mannerism and its establishment as a central style of the High Renaissance. In all these works, Michelangelo's creativity and skill can be recognized, as well as his influences—the greatest of which is da Vinci, who had returned to Florence in 1500 and become acquainted with the 25-year-old Michelangelo.

After completing *David*, Michelangelo skyrocketed in popularity and began working on several ambitious projects in Florence. But he never managed to finish any of them. This was because he was approached by Pope Julius II, who invited the artist to Rome to work on a tomb that would consist of up to forty large statues. Due to political complications in the region, however, which included the turbulent relations between Italian states, this project never began. Michelangelo left Rome for a time, only to return in 1508 to start working on his undisputed magnum opus in painting—the ceiling of the Sistine Chapel. The Sistine Chapel was an integral part of the Vatican Palace, where many ceremonies were conducted. But its main part had already been completely designed, so Michelangelo was to paint a relatively less important room. The initial plan envisioned by the pope and his associates was to devote each of the twelve segments of the ceiling to a depiction of each of the Twelve Apostles. However, after Michelangelo agreed to start working, he applied his own vision to the plan—leading to the creation of one of the most legendary works to this day.

Michelangelo did not completely abandon the pope's vision, though he moved it to the sides of the ceiling. Instead of depicting the apostles, he painted seven prophets and five female sybils from classical mythology on the sides, devoting the central part of the ceiling to the nine scenes of his choosing from Genesis. Three stories were about the creation of the world, three about Adam and Eve, and three about Noah. The corners were filled with other biblical figures from the forty generations before Christ. This colossal work took nearly five years to complete, and Michelangelo worked on it alone, which amplified the difficulty of the job even more.

Michelangelo's idea behind the narrative structure of the ceiling was drastically different from the pope's idea, which saw the ceiling as a potential bridge between the scenes of the Old and New Testaments that were depicted on the walls of the Chapel. The apostles were exactly thought to represent this link in the best way. Michelangelo, however, did not focus on depicting virtuous, devoted apostles to emphasize the biblical sense of goodness they represented. Instead, humanity's disgrace can be identified as the overarching theme of the ceiling. Contrary to what one might initially think, this is a humanist conception at its heart.

Renaissance humanism was not only about depicting man with all his inherently good qualities; it was also about identifying the bad qualities of humanity and, in this way, underlining the innate ability of humans to improve and overcome them. This was Michelangelo's vision. Through his characters and scenes, he wished to portray some of the worst things in the Bible, signifying the flaws of humanity and that it could only be saved by Jesus. Even though the physiques of his characters are all reminiscent of the maximum amount of perfection possible, as was the convention in the Renaissance and in antiquity, Michelangelo did not necessarily make his characters noble, virtuous, or stoic. Instead, the faces of characters in individual paintings are full of mystery and sadness. This is the case, for example, with Adam, in the arguably most famous piece from the ceiling—*The Creation of Adam*. The physiques are near perfection, but the emotion is almost always negative and full of grief. Uncertainty is a central theme and gives the whole composition a unique style. Michelangelo's stylistic decisions for his work in the Sistine Chapel were instrumental in the full-fledged development of Mannerism.

An image of the ceiling of the Sistine Chapel

Antoine Taveneaux, CC BY-SA 3.0 <https://creativecommons.org/licenses/by-sa/3.0>, via Wikimedia Commons; https://commons.wikimedia.org/wiki/File:Sistine_Chapel_ceiling_02_(brightened).jpg

After completing the ceiling of the Sistine Chapel, Michelangelo's career only accelerated further, though that is not to say there were no speed bumps on the road. For example, having finally obtained funding from Pope Julius II to work on the tomb, originally commissioned by the pope in 1505, Michelangelo was soon left disappointed as funding for the project disappeared with the pope's death in 1513. His best work from this project that survived is *Moses,* clearly a Mannerist sculpture with an exaggerated physique and facial expressions. Michelangelo's deep understanding of human anatomy also shows in this work. Later, until the mid-1530s, Michelangelo would be employed by Pope Leo X— the son of Lorenzo de' Medici (a fact that signifies the influence of the Medici and the political turbulence of Renaissance Italy)—and his successor, Pope Clement VII. Mostly spending time in Florence, Michelangelo devoted much of his time to working on the design of the Medici tomb and chapel. He also created most of his architectural designs during this time, once again expressing the best of his unique, Mannerist style and demonstrating his knowledge of military technology when he helped with the fortifications of Florence.

In 1534, Michelangelo returned to Rome at the request of Pope Paul III and would also return to fresco painting after about twenty-five years since the completion of the ceiling of the Sistine Chapel. This time, he was to paint the Chapel's end wall. The topic was the Last Judgment. Perhaps the very last of his greatest works, *The Last Judgement* is painted in a style completely different from the ceiling. By the time of its painting, Michelangelo had fully embraced Mannerism, which can clearly be seen from the excessive quality and quantity of figures, all with exaggerated physiques, depicted in the fresco. Pictured in the center of the giant fresco is Christ, raising his right arm as if to save all who are depicted on his right and lowering his left arm to damn all those on his left. Combining a multitude of biblical characters while fusing in mythical (or pagan) elements like Charon in the bottom right, who is ferrying the damned souls to Hell, *The Last Judgment* might at first be overwhelming to the viewer. There is so much going on that, at first, it seems as if the fresco lacks structure. But as the eye explores the genius of Michelangelo, the dynamism and multiple narratives of the fresco are instantly outlined. The over-exposed physiques of its characters fuse in seamlessly with the relatively simpler colors than those used on the ceiling of the Chapel. Even more impressive, Michelangelo was sixty years old when he painted the fresco.

The Last Judgment by Michelangelo
https://commons.wikimedia.org/wiki/File:Last_Judgement_(Michelangelo).jpg

In his final years, Michelangelo almost completely focused on architecture, designing such important parts of the city of Rome as the dome of St. Peter's Basilica and portions of the Capitol Square. Though he would not live long enough to see his ambitious, grandiose projects fully completed, his plans would be gradually fulfilled after his death and still dazzle viewers. Made illustrious during his lifetime, Michelangelo is rightfully considered one of the greatest artists of all time due to the sheer magnitude of his work and the influence of his style that would last for generations. His compositions are some of the most unique in the world and perfectly capture the spirit of the Renaissance. Grand and sophisticated, Michelangelo remains the ultimate star artist of the Renaissance.

Raphael and the Flexibility of Renaissance Art

The artist considered the third "giant" of the High Renaissance is Raphaello Santi, better known as Raphael. Born in 1483 in the Duchy of Urbino, Raphael was the youngest contemporary of the three but had a much shorter career due to his early death in 1520. He became interested in art through his father, a relatively unsuccessful painter who knew many artists in the city. Raphael eventually went to the city of Perugia to study painting. Although the art scene in Urbino and Perugia was not as developed as in other larger Italian cities like Florence or Rome, young Raphael would be very much influenced by his idols from these cities, discovering their work at a young age. Still, by 1500, his apprenticeship in Perugia had ended, and he had made quite a name for his talent and enthusiasm for painting. Around the same time, he became acquainted with an already-established Renaissance artist, Pietro Perugino, who gave a lot of advice to Raphael when it came to perfecting his painting techniques and later became a big source of inspiration for him.

Raphael completed his *Marriage of the Virgin* in 1504 for the church of San Francesco in the province of Perugia. Painting in oil on a round-headed panel, Raphael seemed to be greatly influenced by the work of his superior, whose *Marriage of the Virgin* is very similar. Following the same stylistic and narrative choices as Perugino, Raphael's painting nevertheless appears more advanced in almost every way, especially in the characters' facial expressions. The temple in the background indicates that, by this time, Raphael had already mastered the manipulation of perspective, something that gave his painting a much more dynamic and completed feeling. The relationship between the architecture in the background and the characters in the foreground is also reminiscent of Perugino's style. This would be an aspect Raphael would only further advance in his later paintings.

Marriage of the Virgin *by Raphael*
https://commons.wikimedia.org/wiki/File:Raffaello_-_Spozalizio_-_Web_Gallery_of_Art.jpg

Marriage of the Virgin by Pietro Perugino
https://commons.wikimedia.org/wiki/File:Pietro_Perugino_cat66.jpg

Another iconic painting of Raphael from this time is his *Vision of the Knight*, completed around the same time as *Marriage*. A perfect example of the importance of symmetry in painting, the painting is split in the middle by a narrow tree. The sleeping knight lying in the center is thought to be ancient Roman general Scipio, who, according to Cicero's accounts, had to choose between Virtue and Pleasure, represented by the two women on either side. Virtue, on the left side, is much more stern and robust, holding a sword and a book. The background on her side is more rocky and hard, emphasizing the difficulty Scipio would encounter in pursuing this quality. On the other hand, Pleasure is depicted with more liberty, wearing a looser robe, her hair visible, and holding a flower. In a way, the two ladies are not depicted in a contest with one another since the symbolic objects that they are holding can be attained in synthesis. The sword signifies knighthood and honor, the book stands for knowledge and wisdom, and a flower represents love—all qualities necessary for an ideal person, consistent with the humanist vision. With great use of various shades of blue, mastery of perspective as seen from the seamless fusion of the background with the characters in the front, a symmetry that is obtained by splitting the painting in two, and the narrative and symbolic background the painting represents, *Vision of the Knight* is one of the most perfect examples of Renaissance art and signifies the genius Raphael had managed to achieve in his early years.

Raphael's Vision of a Knight
https://commons.wikimedia.org/wiki/File:RAFAEL_-_Sue%C3%B1o_del_Caballero_(National_Gallery_de_Londres,_1504._%C3%93leo_sobre_tabla,_17_x_17_cm).jpg

Already considered one of the brightest of his generation, Raphael also completed *St. Michael* and *Three Graces* during his time in Perugia, but it soon became clear that he was ready to expand his horizons. The move to Florence served this purpose. Drawn to the center of Italian art thanks to his admiration for Leonardo and Michelangelo, he explored new technical and narrative styles pioneered by these become visible in

Raphael's works almost instantly after his decision to move to Florence. A series of Madonnas he completed throughout the late first decade of the 1500s are a testament to this. Painting the Virgin became a staple of Raphael synonymous with his style and personality, and the pure and uncomplicated way he depicted the Madonna marveled his contemporaries. Managing to capture her innocence as described in the Bible, Raphael's Madonna was also intimate and virtuous, a fundamental aspect of Renaissance painting. His colors became darker and his shading more profound owing to the influence of Leonardo. In his *Deposition of Christ*, completed in 1507, Raphael shows his deep understanding of the human body and paints a dynamic picture full of story and character. The *Deposition* perfectly captures the essence of the biblical scene, combining the grievous expressions on the faces of the lamenters and the lifeless expression of Christ, creating a complicated and dynamic scene full of chaos.

Deposition of Christ *by Raphael*
https://commons.wikimedia.org/wiki/File:Raffaello,_pala_baglioni,_deposizione.jpg

In 1508, Raphael was brought to Rome by Julius II, and the last twelve years of his career were when he truly reached his peak. Architect Donato Bramante suggested Raphael (still a relatively young artist at that time) to the pope, who, as mentioned, had ambitious plans for the decoration of the Vatican and the improvement of the public spaces in Rome. He commissioned Rafael to start painting the walls of the papal apartments, known as the Stanza.

Raphael's work in the Stanza della Segnatura is considered his magnum opus. The four walls of the chamber all have frescoes by Raphael. His *Disputation of the Sacrament* is an amazing piece of work that depicts Christ and other biblical and historical figures disputing Christian doctrine. It is Raphael's attempt at representing individuals who had been most important in developing the Christian religion as it was and is meant to symbolize the triumph and superiority of the Catholic Church. Christ is, of course, at the center, flanked on either side by the Virgin Mary and John the Baptist and other important biblical characters like the apostles, King David, Moses, John the Evangelist, and Abraham. A multitude of historical characters are also pictured below Christ. They are some of the most vital theologians from the history of Christianity, such as St. Augustine and Ambrose, several popes (including Pope Julius II), Jerome, and St. Thomas Aquinas. The painting also includes depictions of Savonarola, a Florentine friar and revolutionary who was the theocratic ruler of Florence for a short time, Dante (for his contributions to the fusion of Christianity and classicism), and Aristotle—one of the biggest inspirations of medieval scholarship. Finally, to pay homage to his mentor, Raphael also included Bramante, making for an eclectic mix of individuals. He believed they were most crucial—not only for the development of human thought and understanding of Christian doctrine but also for the thriving of the Church and religion as a whole. This latter understanding of the Church's position was characteristic of High Renaissance when it became the main patron of arts in Italy.

Disputation of the Sacrament *by Raphael*
https://commons.wikimedia.org/wiki/File:Disputa_del_Sacramento_(Rafael).jpg

Raphael's *School of Athens,* on the opposite wall of the *Disputation,* is commonly considered his magnum opus. A homage to classical scholarship and his contemporaries, the fresco is a celebration of philosophy and knowledge unlike any other. The center of the fresco is occupied by Plato and Aristotle, the central figures for Raphael in the development of philosophic thought, each representing their own ideological bases. To the left, Plato is depicted as an older man pointing to the sky, hinting at his understanding of the world of ideas, holding his *Timaeus.* Aristotle, depicted as a younger but still a mature person, is gesturing downwards—emphasizing his main perception of particulars and holding his *Nicomachean Ethics.* The two central figures of the fresco are surrounded by other important members who have contributed to the development and perfection of secular knowledge, including Anaximander, Diogenes, Socrates, Parmenides, Zeno, Epicurus, Pythagoras, and Archimedes. The fresco also includes depictions of people such as Alexander the Great, Ptolemy, and Zoroaster, as well as a personal portrait of Raphael, who is looking directly at the viewer from the bottom right corner. The man writing in the middle is also supposedly Michelangelo, depicted by Raphael as Heraclitus. Greek mathematician Euclid, who is bent over and measuring on the right, is supposed to be Bramante. A perfect culmination of the High Renaissance, *The School of Athens* is a beautiful fresco that points to Raphael's fascination with the individuals depicted in it. Combining this sense of admiration with a masterful expression of perspective and lighting, *The School of Athens* remains perhaps the most celebrated of Raphael's works.

School of Athens *by Raphael*
https://en.wikipedia.org/wiki/File:%22The_School_of_Athens%22_by_Raffaello_Sanzio_da_Urbino.jpg

Commissioned by the pope, Raphael was also instructed to paint the Stanza di Eliodoro, and the artist's work there is a step forward in his ability to express narrative and technique. The contents of the frescoes in this Stanza are far more straightforward than those depicted in the other, lacking the allegorical and symbolic meanings of *The School of Athens* and *Disputation* but nevertheless excelling in form and storytelling. *The Mass at Bolsena, Liberation of St. Peter, Expulsion of Heliodorus,* and *Meeting of Leo the Great and Attila* all display Raphael's mastery of color and shading techniques, owing to the influences of Michelangelo and Leonardo. The manipulation of light and the transition from darker to lighter parts in these frescoes are excellently accomplished, and the fusion of multiple sources of light only amplifies their effects on the viewer. In addition, paintings the artist completed around the same time as his work in the Stanzas, such as *Triumph of Galatea*, demonstrate Raphael's understanding of the human body and may even be considered early Mannerism. Still, the characters in these works are shown to be glorious and epic, with an emphasis on clearly showing their perfect physical attributes. At the same time, Raphael also painted some of the most subtle and gentle works in his career, reminiscent of his early work. For example, in his hailed *Sistine Madonna*, completed in 1513, Raphael recaptures the serenity and innocence that characterized his early career. However, this depiction of Madonna is far richer in color and more interesting in narrative than his previous work. It seems as if *Sistine Madonna* is a culmination of the artist's exploration of the theme, as his other depictions of Madonna from this period, such as *Alba Madonna* (1508) and *Madonna di Foligno* (1510), serve as preludes to this work.

Sistine Madonna, *Raphael*
https://commons.wikimedia.org/wiki/File:RAFAEL_-_Madonna_Sixtina_(Gem%C3%A4ldegalerie_Alter_Meister,_Dresden,_1513-14,_%C3%93leo_sobre_lienzo,_265_x_196_cm).jpg

What can be observed from Raphael's move to Rome is the fact that he often worked on multiple projects at once. Despite his relatively short lifespan, he managed to leave behind a substantial body of work that is celebrated to this day. In fact, in the last decade of his life, he became so popular thanks to papal patronage and his excellence that he emerged as a prominent portrait painter in the city. His portrait of *Baldassare Castiglione*, completed in 1516, is a great example of the flexibility of Raphael's artistic ability. He could paint grand, majestic biblical or mythological scenes full of complex characters that synthesized to form a complicated narrative. In addition, he could also capture sophistication, purity, and innocence all at once in his characters, evidenced in his various paintings of Madonna and the portraits he completed in his later career. In fact, Raphael's amazing ability to switch effortlessly between such drastic styles of painting can be observed in the final years of his life with his last work, *Transfiguration*, which was commissioned by Cardinal Giulio de' Medici (soon to be Pope Clement VII) in 1517. Having a pyramid structure, *Transfiguration* combines shade manipulation and color contrast, emphasizing the main idea of the narrative depicted in the painting. The painting has been interpreted as Raphael's first real Mannerist work, and some art historians even consider the style to be more reminiscent of the Baroque period, which would come a couple of hundred years after the Renaissance.

Transfiguration, *Raphael*
https://commons.wikimedia.org/wiki/File:Transfiguration_Raphael.jpg

All in all, Raphael is rightfully considered among the three biggest names of Italian High Renaissance art alongside Leonardo da Vinci and Michelangelo. His supreme ability to combine the serenity and grandeur of his characters with a creative way of conveying narrative and symbolism in his paintings rightfully makes him one of the most brilliant minds of the time. Hailed during his lifetime as an extremely talented and tasteful individual, Raphael enjoyed papal patronage in Rome and even participated in overseeing larger architectural projects undertaken by Leo X. His untimely death from a fever at the age of thirty-seven came as a tragedy to the contemporary Italian society that was familiar with his genius. Raphael's funeral mass was organized in the Vatican, and the great artist was buried in the Pantheon of Rome, a gesture of the eternal city eternalizing one of its most accomplished individuals.

Chapter Five – Renaissance Science and Technology

Shifting Paradigms

The Scientific Revolution was an equally impactful part of the Renaissance as the cultural advancements that took place in Europe increasingly after the 14th century. Of course, it is important to remember that all the things we have mentioned and are about to cover were taking place around the same time. The developments in science and technology resulted from the birth of humanist thought and a renewed will to explore, which began in Italy and then spread further to the rest of Europe. As previously emphasized, the biggest change that gradually took place in the minds of the most educated members of the otherwise uneducated European population was a fundamental paradigm shift. With a new desire to better understand nature and become its master—a humanist conception at its core—Renaissance scientists managed to make revolutionary findings. Together, they contributed to changing the existing Christian understanding of how the world worked and started the long process of a paradigm shift in the medieval era, which would reach its peak with the Age of Enlightenment a few centuries after the height of the Renaissance.

Interestingly, with the rediscovery of ancient texts, people also regained access to a lot of previous scientific knowledge in different fields, such as astronomy. Ancient Greeks and Roman scientists had speculated about the design of the world and had used several different means to obtain the knowledge they believed would confirm their findings. The scientific method, though partially present in ancient Greece in the works of Aristotle, for example, was still underdeveloped. By the 11th century, it had been advanced mostly in the Arabic world, during the Islamic Golden Age, where science and mathematics were much more developed than in Europe. In the Muslim world, experimentation had slowly begun to be understood as a reliable method of testing theories and obtaining knowledge. Arab mathematicians, physicists, and physicians, such as Ibn al-Haytham (Alhazen) and Ibn Sina (Avicenna), developed the scientific method from its applications in classical antiquity. Crucially, this happened because they had access to classical literature and translated it into Arabic. Alhazen and Avicenna knew of Aristotle, Epicurus, Democritus, and other ancient Greek philosophers and theorists and built upon their knowledge.

With the rediscovery of ancient knowledge and the gradual diffusion of knowledge from the East to Europe, the scientists of the 12th and 13th centuries started to get acquainted with all these conceptions. The scientific method (the version applied at the time) was gaining more and more traction. Unfortunately, just like everything else at the time, the Black Death stopped much of this move forward when it wiped out millions of people in Europe, literate and illiterate. Still, with the Renaissance, increasing interest was shown in obtaining knowledge, and several contemporary developments accelerated the spread and the desire to obtain knowledge.

The Printing Press

A monumental technological breakthrough in the mid-15th century changed the way Europeans accessed and perceived knowledge: the development of the printing press by a German goldsmith, Johannes Gutenberg. By the time Gutenberg completed his version of the printing press around 1440, the Early Renaissance and the socioeconomic progress it brought had made it almost necessary for information to be produced and transferred more quickly than before. Scholarship had developed considerably with the rediscovery of classical literature and the new writings of medieval scholars motivated to contribute to the existing body of knowledge with their own discoveries. Translation and copying, however, took time and were mainly done by the clergy in the monasteries and cathedrals. But demand and interest were very high among the public, especially those in the higher classes with more means of acquiring knowledge.

In the 15th century, however, several other important developments inspired Gutenberg to create his printing machine. First was the introduction of Chinese-type paper to Europe from the East through the Arabic world. The Arabs had close trade contact with the distant Chinese civilization and had learned the craft of papermaking from them before the Renaissance flourished in Europe. In Europe, several different presses had existed from ancient times, mostly used for making wine or manufacturing cloth. Gutenberg aimed to fuse the two together, creating perhaps the most revolutionary piece of technology in Europe since the wheel.

The design was relatively simple. Gutenberg's printing press began with creating metal pieces for each character, punctuation mark, or symbol. These pieces were made using typecasting, a method where molten metal was poured into molds with the reverse image of each character. Once the metal type pieces were ready, they were arranged correctly on a composing stick. The compositor, the main person behind the process, assembled the type in a mirrored manner, reading the text backward. To apply ink, the typeset text was carefully transferred from the composing stick to the form, a large frame placed on the flat bed of the press. The ink, which was oil-based and sticky (and also developed by Gutenberg), was applied to the raised surfaces of the metal type using inkballs or ink rollers. Next, a sheet of slightly damp paper was positioned over the inked type by hand or using a wooden frame called a tympan. This ensured that the ink would transfer well onto the paper. To initiate the printing process, the compositor pushed a lever connected to a screw-operated platen. The platen exerted significant force when pressed down, creating an impression by making contact with the inked type and transferring the ink onto the paper. After the impression was made, the platen was raised, and the printed sheet was removed. This process was repeated for each sheet, allowing for the production of multiple copies of the same text.

The first book ever printed was the Bible, known as the Gutenberg Bible, and only a handful of copies of the very first edition survives today, all of which are believed to be extremely valuable. A direct consequence of Gutenberg's invention was the printing revolution—the exponential spread of printing throughout Europe that contributed greatly to the circulation of knowledge and different ideas, only accelerating the process started by the Renaissance. Not only that, but the printing press led to the creation of thousands of different jobs as more cities adopted the press in pursuit of utilizing it to its full benefit. By the end of the 15th century, up to 300 cities in Western Europe had a printing press. Germany, Low Countries, and Northern Italy especially benefitted due to their decentralized but highly urban political structures. This resulted in a drastic increase in book production and, consequently, increased literacy rates throughout Europe, which had circular, complementary effects. According to some estimates, by 1500, Europe had about two hundred million copies of different books. The printing revolution also gave way to the subsequent scientific revolution, which would take Europe by storm in the next century-and-a-half and produce some of the most marvelous findings in the Renaissance.

The Scientific Renaissance

The Scientific Renaissance applies to a period from the mid-15th century to the mid-17th century. At this time, most advances in astronomy, anatomy, mathematics, physics, medicine, and other natural sciences took place in Europe, ultimately ushering in an even more sophisticated and advanced Age of Enlightenment, as mentioned. The Scientific Renaissance was a gradual process. Its prelude was the rediscovery of ancient texts, which caused a renewed, increased interest in these fields. As more scholars started to flesh out their theories regarding the different aspects of science, the invention of the printing press would help greatly in the diffusion of knowledge among them and the public. The result was a new spirit of the scientific community and the "formal" establishment of such a community in the first place.

The Scientific Renaissance included multiple paradigm shifts. One already mentioned was the development of the scientific method and a more coherent theory of reliably obtaining knowledge. The conceptions of Copernicus, Galileo, Kepler, Harvey, and later Newton, for example, resulted in a gradual move away from the traditional, medieval way of understanding the world, the most obvious characteristic of which was placing the Earth in the center of the universe. Contrary to popular perception, however, what took place was not a "scientific revolution"—a term that has been applied to describe scientific progress and discoveries from the late 16th to the 18th centuries. We must understand that change took place step by step. As ancient knowledge was being rediscovered, the theories being developed by Renaissance scientists and scholars were initially only known to a handful of people. Crucially, the Polish astronomer and mathematician Nicolaus Copernicus first proposed the revolutionary heliocentric model of the solar system, challenging the prevailing perception of the Earth. His seminal work, recorded in *De Revolutionibus Orbium Coelestium* (On the Rotation of the Celestial Spheres), laid the foundation for a new and deeper understanding of the universe and revolutionized scientific thinking.

Though Copernicus was challenged by the religious authorities, who correctly perceived the proposed model of the Earth as dangerous to their power, the works of other scientists, like Galileo, reconfirmed the concepts of the Polish astronomer. Galileo Galilei is another monumental figure of the Renaissance. An Italian scientist of the 16th-17th centuries, Galileo made outstanding contributions to the fields of physics and astronomy, as well as to the development of scientific instruments. Most notably, he improved the telescope to make new observations, such as discovering Jupiter's moons and observing the phases of Venus. Galileo's work further substantiated the heliocentric theory and cast doubt on the prevailing Aristotelian cosmology. German astronomer Johannes Kepler, who formulated his three laws of planetary motion, also expanded on Galileo's work. These laws provided a mathematical explanation for the motion of the planets around the Sun and further strengthened our scientific understanding of celestial mechanics. Still, the Catholic Church was also discontented with Galileo and denounced his science as heresy.

In addition, we have already mentioned the breakthroughs in the field of anatomy by Leonardo da Vinci, who was partly motivated to depict the human physique as perfectly as he could in his artistic works. However, medicine and anatomy also advanced greatly during the Renaissance in Northern Europe. Flemish physician Andreas Vesalius, for example, revolutionized the study of anatomy with his influential set of books *De Humani Corporis Fabrica Libri Septim*, emphasizing the importance of direct observation and careful dissection, correcting longstanding anatomical misconceptions and making great strides in our understanding of the human body.

Overall, the history of Renaissance science marked a significant shift from reliance on ancient authority to direct observation, experimentation, and mathematical reasoning. This paradigm shift laid the foundation for the scientific revolution that unfolded over the following centuries, ushering in a new era of scientific inquiry and discovery. The Renaissance catalyzed the development of modern scientific methods and knowledge, enabling humanity to broaden its understanding of the natural world and embark on an extraordinary journey of exploration and innovation. More fundamentally, it also weakened the Catholic Church's authority since it was becoming apparent that the Church could not effectively combat the claims of new science with its old, strict, and doctrine-based views. This was especially prevalent as more and more people became literate and had new means of obtaining books. The decline of the Church's influence was accelerated by another greatly important development of the Renaissance in the 16th century—namely, the Protestant Revolution.

Chapter Six – The Northern Renaissance

Contextualizing the Northern Renaissance

We must remember that the Renaissance was not confined to Italy. Instead, as time passed, it slowly spread from the peninsula north of the Alps. Some main themes that characterized the movement in Italy were replicated and advanced in the Holy Roman Empire, France, Netherlands, England, and even Poland. The Northern Renaissance built on the intellectual, artistic, and socioeconomic developments of the Italian Renaissance, producing a comparably rich heritage that would influence history for centuries to come.

The context of the Northern Renaissance was highly similar to that of the Italian Renaissance. After the population decline and other associated harms caused by the Black Death, the situation slowly normalized again in Europe. This meant a new wave of migration to the urban areas and, consequently, the development of a more interconnected and prosperous society. One result was the centralization of most political entities north of the Alps. For example, full-fledged kingdoms with more clearly defined borders and structures started to emerge from the chaotic remnants of the Middle Ages in France and England. In the Holy Roman Empire, the political structure was still very much decentralized. However, the growing influence of the Austrian Habsburg dynasty was beginning to show. In fact, by the 16th century, the Habsburgs directly controlled many of the German lands in Central

Europe and were kings of Spain and suzerains of the Dutch city-states. International borders had started to loosely resemble their modern versions, though constant wars ensured that the influence between international actors was heavily contested. Higher levels of urbanization and increased trade in Northern Europe challenged the trading monopoly of the Italian states in the Mediterranean. Because a new centralized Russian state had also started to take shape, the goods from Asia could reach the northern markets through Russia much more easily, not only through the south.

In turn, the growth of cities resulted in a growing demand for new services and goods, further accelerating economic growth. In turn, economic prosperity was the prerequisite for fostering the cultural and intellectual needs of the people, which were also aided by existing trends in Italy. More universities were founded and matured in the 15th and 16th centuries, becoming centers of idea exchange. Ancient texts that had fascinated Italians, Greeks, and Arabs for centuries (increasing numbers of which were slowly being uncovered in the 14th and 15th centuries) were scattered around in the cathedrals north of the Alps—the main repository of knowledge in this region, as well. Still, these developments came about half a century or so later than they had in Italy. A growing network of scholars, merchants, and artists contributed to the diffusion of these ideas, eventually resulting in the development of Northern Humanism, which owed a lot to Italian humanist thought but also had its own distinct character. Finally, Gutenberg's printing press greatly accelerated knowledge exchange in the rest of Europe, producing a thriving culture that certainly rivaled Italian Renaissance.

Perhaps the most influential figure who contributed the most to the development of Northern humanist thought was Erasmus of Rotterdam. Born in Rotterdam, Holland, in the late 1460s, Erasmus became a prominent humanist, theologian, and scholar, and his ideas and achievements laid the foundation for important advances in a wide variety of fields. Erasmus' role in the revival of classical scholarship in Northern Europe was immense. Erasmus' most notable early work, *Adagia,* published in 1500, is a collection of proverbs and sayings from Greek and Latin sources. This work proved Erasmus' erudition and encouraged the adoption of classical wisdom in contemporary society, as it was perceived to be timeless knowledge that anyone could use in any situation. As a prominent scholar and advocate of what humanism stood for, Erasmus believed in the transformative power of education and defended it. He emphasized the importance of classical language, literature, and critical thinking in curriculum. Erasmus earned a reputation as a prolific author of textbooks and educational treatises, such as *De Copia* (1512), which taught his students the art of rhetoric and effective communication. His ideas influenced educational institutions throughout Europe and laid the foundations for modern educational practice.

Though Erasmus was a devout Catholic, he also advocated for a return to the original teachings of Christianity, believing in the importance of personal piety and true Christianity. His most famous work, *In Praise of Folly* (1509), satirically criticized corruption and excesses within the Catholic Church. He was one of the main Renaissance scholars to deeply study the Bible to better understand Christian doctrine. More importantly, in 1516, he concentrated his findings and interpretations of the Scriptures into a new, translated edition of the New Testament known as the *Novum Instrumentum*. By providing original texts, Erasmus hoped to promote a more informed and critical understanding of Christian doctrine. For him, the essence of Christianity was not in blindly following the directions of the Church or its authorities when it came to prayer, for example. Instead, he stressed the need to apply critical reasoning to doctrine, in line with the rest of the Renaissance movement. With the Church's monopoly over the dissemination of religious knowledge, common people could not truly interpret the meaning of Christianity for themselves, Erasmus believed. He thought that intellectual dialogue and understanding between different religious and cultural groups was essential to the progress of society, emphasizing peace, harmony, and tolerance. Eventually, Erasmus' emphasis on personal faith and biblical scholarship laid the foundation for the later Protestant Reformation, which would directly affect the lives of millions of Europeans.

The Reformation

Though it is often regarded as its own phenomenon, the Protestant Reformation can certainly be regarded as one of the most fundamental developments of the Late Renaissance period, directly influenced by the intellectual and social dynamics of the early stages of the movement. A revolution in the 16th-century Catholic world that eventually resulted in the creation of a new branch of Christianity distinct from both Catholicism and Eastern Orthodoxy, the Reformation had far-reaching implications. Protestantism (represented by a mix of denominations) is still the fastest-growing Christian movement in the world.

German theologian Martin Luther is often considered the main man behind the Protestant Reformation. However, it is important to understand that the movement took shape gradually and had different centers and leaders in Western Europe. In the Swiss city of Geneva, for example, John Calvin led the Protestant movement against the Catholic Church and is also considered an instrumental figure of the Reformation. This chapter will briefly cover the history of the Reformation in the context of the Renaissance and how exactly this development was caused by the intellectual and cultural drive for rebirth that was characteristic of the period.

When looking at the Reformation through the lens of the Renaissance, two things must be acknowledged. The first is the influence of Erasmus' writings and his study of Christian texts on the leaders of the Reformation (which we will get to later when we discuss what motivated Luther, Calvin, and others to go against the authority of the Catholic Church). The second is the state of Catholicism in the 16th century, which is directly connected to the developments in the Early and High Renaissance periods. As already mentioned, the influence of the Catholic Church as the most important institution of Europe grew with the Renaissance movement. The regional churches of different European kingdoms were very powerful but still subject to the authority of the papacy, which controlled a lot of land and resources in Central Italy. The structure of the Church was very centralized and hierarchical, with clear distinctions between the different ranks of the clergy and their roles. The papacy was also heavily involved in the political matters of the world at the time, viewing itself as a sort of international arbiter. Indeed, when rulers were endorsed by the Church and had the religious authorities on their side, their power was much more apparent and present. This was because the meaning of life for an average low-class medieval or Renaissance person was set by the principles of religion. To the laypeople, the Church was their main spiritual guide, and understandably so. Most people were illiterate and uneducated, content with following the rules the Church authorities set out for them. Living by the rules and standards of the Church was comfortable, even if problems existed in the fundamental nature of the Church and its roles—something that would be outlined by Luther and other leaders of the Protestant movement.

With the development of humanist thought that emphasized critical thinking and increased the spirit of inquiry, scholars started to identify aspects of the Catholic Church they found problematic. At its core, the overarching idea the leaders of the Reformation had was a gradual move away from the strictly hierarchical nature of the Church and a return to the doctrinal basis—something that had been outlined by Erasmus of Rotterdam and others.

Among the important criticisms that would be stressed later was the intrinsic corruption in the Church. The sale of indulgences was one of the problems. In the medieval era, one could approach a priest and ask for forgiveness for sins, paying them a certain amount of money for the sins to be absolved. Indulgence could also be directed at releasing the individual from the judgment of purgatory—a state of suffering after death where the souls of sinners would answer for their sins, according to Catholic teaching. The Catholic Church supposedly obtained a large portion of its income this way. When the profit from selling indulgences combined with instances of nepotism, the illegitimacy and incompetence of the clergy, whose interpretation and teaching of doctrine was dubious, and the special privileges churchmen all over Europe enjoyed, a sense of protest was born among those who recognized the nature of the problems.

Moreover, by the 1500s, as we have seen from the lavish and ambitious projects undertaken by the popes, the wealth of the Church had skyrocketed. More money meant more influence on political affairs, which, in turn, meant more ways of getting more money. Overall, according to the protesters, it was a fundamentally flawed system that had gone corrupt and diverted from its roots. The Catholic Church needed some changes.

Although efforts had been made centuries before the Renaissance to implement changes in the Church, October 31, 1517, is usually considered the "beginning" of the Protestant Reformation. It is a significant date because it was when Martin Luther—a religious scholar and professor—nailed his Ninety-Five Theses on the door of Castle Church in Wittenberg, Germany. In the Theses, Luther outlined the main problems with the present state of the Church. He attacked the religious authorities for permitting such a flawed system to persist for centuries and exploit the lives of ordinary people. He also proposed changes that could save the state of the Church, emphasizing salvation by faith alone (*sola fide*) and the authority of Scripture (*sola scriptura*).

Clearly influenced by Erasmus, Luther's main idea was that the true meaning of Christianity was in the Holy Scriptures and that the way it was taught in contemporary churches was fundamentally different from how it was intended to be taught in the ancient texts. Luther's ideas spread quickly throughout the main urban centers of Germany (Holy Roman Empire) thanks to their effective reproduction by the printing press. The reaction from Church authorities came quickly—they denounced him as a heretic and even excommunicated Luther in 1521. However, reform also seemed attractive to many individuals, including political and religious figures, who began implementing them in their local congregations. In this matter, the decentralized political structure of the Holy Roman Empire came in handy. Since local princes held the most authority in their chiefdoms, principalities, city-states, or baronies, they could implement the changes however they wanted and escape imperial or papal authority. Frederick III the Wise, the Elector of Saxony, was a political leader who protected Luther from the papal authorities by hiding him in the Wartburg Castle, where the theologian continued to immerse himself in religious research in late 1521. Over the next few years, Luther worked on his translation of the Bible into German to make it more accessible to the masses. His version was published and reprinted all throughout the German-speaking world. Over time, more and more parts of Europe embraced various forms of Protestantism thanks to the rapid dissemination of ideas that many found attractive and relevant.

Other important reformers include John Calvin, a Frenchman who had fled his country of origin for Switzerland, where religious freedoms were much more respected than in France. In Geneva, he became further acquainted with Luther's ideas and agreed with many of them, eventually developing his own version, known as Calvinism. Over time, Calvinism would become the main Protestant movement in most of Switzerland, the Netherlands, Scotland, and parts of France, centered on its understanding of the doctrine of predestination. Huldrych Zwingli would lead the Protestant movement in Zürich, which eventually merged with Calvin's denomination in the mid-16th century. Together, these versions of Protestant thought emphasized moral discipline and hard work and would emerge as a main foundation for the development of capitalism, as it would be later outlined by sociologist Max Webber. More radical versions of Protestantism, such as Anabaptism, also developed and were adopted to varying degrees in different parts of

Europe. The key difference with Anabaptists was that they rejected the conventional practice of infant baptism, believing it was not mentioned in the original Scripture. As time passed, more individual theologians and scholars would propose subtle changes to previously-accepted forms of Protestantism, leading to the creation of more denominations and what scholars have deemed the "democratization" of religion. Based on the main idea of interpreting the essence of the Holy Scriptures as best as possible without the restrictions and proposed interpretations of the Catholic Church, Protestantism flourished in most of Germany, the Netherlands, Scotland, and Scandinavia. The Catholic Church's influence, on the other hand, was mostly maintained in Italy, where its presence was the strongest, as well as in France and Spain.

The social and political implications of the Reformation would be apparent centuries after the end of the Renaissance. First, it triggered many religious wars on the European continent, with coalitions of Catholics and Protestants going toe-to-toe to impose their beliefs on the other. The Thirty Years' War, for example, is one such conflict, greatly altering the power dynamics among the European powers in the 1600s and contributing to the spread or containment of Protestantism around Europe. Protestantism also became a main factor in England's subsequent political turmoil, leading to King Henry VIII's decision to abandon Catholicism and instead "found" his own version of Protestantism, known as Anglicanism. Secondly, it led to the conflicts of the English civil war, which would cement Anglicanism as the official religion of the state, combining the role of the head of state and church, which is still a central aspect of the British monarchy today. More fundamentally, Protestantism led to the emergence of diverse religious beliefs and practices within Europe and the rise of religious toleration in some areas. Previous church structures and hierarchies would be fully modified to make room for new religious dynamics. All in all, the Reformation would embody the spirit of the Renaissance that stressed an individual interpretation of Scripture and the importance of education, contributing to increased literacy rates and the establishment of schools and universities.

Northern Renaissance Art

The Reformation is just one of the developments that can be considered part of the Northern Renaissance, though its peak took place late in the period and essentially bridged the Late Renaissance with the early stages of the Enlightenment. The Northern Renaissance was full of many cultural achievements just as celebrated as those of the Italian Renaissance. Again, the extensive interconnected nature of Europe in the 15th century contributed greatly to the flourishing of cultural exchange between Italy and Northern Europe. Non-Italian humanist thought and the rediscovery of ancient knowledge also made it so that some of the artistic developments of the Northern Renaissance took place at almost the same time as in Italy.

Hieronymus Bosch, Pieter Bruegel, Jan van Eyck, Albrecht Dürer, Rogier van der Weyden, and Jean Fouquet are among the most recognized names of the Northern Renaissance. The styles they developed sometimes reflected and tried to copy the developments in Italian art and sometimes responded to them. Perhaps the main difference between the two styles is that Northern Renaissance painting did not focus as heavily on religious or mythological themes as Italian Renaissance painting, though both were present during the early stages. Instead, scenes of everyday life were often depicted in Northern Renaissance art. These works, known as "genre scenes" or "genre art," offered a glimpse into the lives of ordinary people, including home environments, landscapes, markets, and interpersonal interactions.

The Northern Renaissance genre scene was distinguished by its naturalistic approach and attention to detail. Artists tried to accurately portray their subjects and capture the nuances of human gestures, expressions, and interactions. They paid special attention to the details of clothing, furniture, household items, and the architectural elements of the spaces depicted. By carefully rendering these elements, the artist created a sense of authenticity and allowed the viewer to connect with the scene on a personal and relatable level. In contrast, Italian Renaissance painting was much grander and more ambitious, often depicting narrative scenery that was difficult to comprehend if the context or title of the work was not known. Instead of showing excerpts from the Bible, ancient mythology, or history or presenting viewers with overwhelming imagery that made a great impression at first glance, northern painters often depicted people of different social classes performing their respective activities, a much subtler approach to conveying the story inside the paintings. They showed the lives of farmers, artisans, merchants, and aristocrats, reflecting the diverse social structure of Flemish, Dutch, and German societies at the time. Scenes of rural life depicted peasants working in the fields, herding cattle, and participating in seasonal events. Street vendors, markets, taverns, and workshops are featured in urban genre scenes, depicting the bustling energy and exuberance of city life. All in all, these subjects were much more relatable for the average viewer.

Narrative storytelling also played an important role in genre scenes in the Northern Renaissance. Artists used these scenes to convey moral messages, fables, or humorous anecdotes. The characters' actions and interactions within the composition were carefully crafted to tell a specific story or capture a moment in the human experience. These stories often reflect the values, customs, and social conditions of the time, providing viewers with insight into the moral, social, and cultural context. A notable example is the work of Pieter Bruegel the Elder. His paintings, such as *Peasant's Wedding* and *Hunters in the Snow*, depict detailed and expansive scenes of peasants engaged in various activities throughout the seasons. Bruegel's work visually documents everyday life and communicates deeper social, cultural, and moral issues. His scenes served as observational representations of reality and vehicles for artistic expression and social criticism. They provided insight into the human experience, capturing the joys, struggles, and oddities of everyday life. By portraying the everyday and familiar, they resonated with viewers and inspired them to reflect on their lives and the world around them.

As we mentioned, to convey this style, great attention to realistically depicting the characters and objects in the paintings was extremely important. So, Northern Renaissance art laid important foundations for the subsequent realism movement in later centuries. Northern Renaissance artists wanted to bring the human being to life, emphasizing anatomical accuracy and natural proportions. They paid close attention to the details of facial features and accurately recorded individual features and expressions. Using light and shadow helped create depth and three-dimensionality and added realism to the characters. Obviously, Italian art was a great influence. The garments and textiles depicted in Northern Renaissance art are meticulously crafted and demonstrate the artists' technical excellence. Fabrics are carefully rendered to reveal intricate patterns, folds, and textures. This attention to detail extended to the depiction of jewelry, accessories, and other decorative elements.

In addition to the human figure, Northern Renaissance artists focused on capturing the natural world with precision and detail. Landscape painting emerged as a major genre, and artists painted landscapes realistically. They paid particular attention to the depiction of vegetation, trees, bodies of water, and atmospheric effects. These landscapes were often sprinkled with symbolic and narrative elements that added layers of meaning to the natural landscape. On the other hand, in the works of some of the most distinguished Italian painters, the focus is rarely directed toward nature; the emphasis is on the paintings' characters. Backgrounds of paintings from the Italian Renaissance are often simple and rarely heavily detailed in contrast to the Northern Renaissance style. This attention to detail also led to the flourishing of still-life painting. Everyday objects such as flowers, fruits, food, and daily necessities were meticulously cared for, and attention was paid to texture, color, and lighting to enhance the sense of realism. The desire for realism and naturalism in Northern Renaissance art went hand-in-hand with the scientific and intellectual developments of the time. Notable artists associated with Northern Renaissance realism and naturalism include Jan van Eyck, Albrecht Dürer, and Hieronymus Bosch.

In turn, a growing interest in individualism, human psychology, and the expression of social status and identity was expressed in the development of portraiture as a prominent genre of the Northern Renaissance. Artists such as Hans Holbein the Younger and Jan van Eyck used meticulous techniques to capture the physical features of a seated person with astonishing accuracy. They emphasized facial features, hair, clothing, and accessories and executed them meticulously. Through their technical skill, they wanted to capture even the tiniest nuances and imperfections, creating a faithful representation of the sitters, combining the realistic aspects with great technique and even scattering symbolic representations of ideas in the paintings. Northern Renaissance portraits were often commissioned by wealthy commoners, clerics, or aristocrats who wanted to assert their social status and transmit a particular image to posterity. They were prominently displayed in private homes, guild halls, or public places and served as visual proof of a model's wealth, influence, and achievements. These portraits also strengthened family ties, social networks, and dynastic legacies. In Italy, however, portrait painting did not flourish to the same level as in the Northern Renaissance.

Thus, rooted in Northern humanism and important regional socio-cultural developments such as the Reformation, the Northern Renaissance developed its own identity independently from the Italian Renaissance. The socio-cultural factors that had resulted in the active patronage of Italian artists were largely absent from the North, most apparent in the Church's authority, which would slowly diminish as the Reformation gained more traction. While Italian artists had the resources to work for years on grand and ambitious projects commissioned by the papacy, this was largely untrue for the Northern painters. In the North, art was commissioned by members of different social classes, making the product more diverse but simple and relatable. This, in turn, meant that the profession of an artist also developed differently than in Italy, emerging as more of a traditional job that made money for the artist instead of a career only fit for the extremely talented minority. This was apparent not only stylistically but also in the dispersion of Northern Renaissance artists in many different places instead of being concentrated in only a handful of cities, as in Italy. Overall, the Northern Renaissance produced some of the most memorable works of art of its time that clearly reflected the socio-cultural and economic factors present in Northern and Central Europe.

English Renaissance

The Renaissance reached England a bit later than the rest of continental Western Europe and stayed there later, until the early 17th century. Still, English social developments that precipitated the move from the medieval way of life and thought to the Renaissance greatly resembled those in Italy and Northern Europe. Thus, to conclude the history of artistic and cultural achievements the Renaissance entailed, it is only fitting to look at how the movement flourished in England. As mentioned earlier, England would be among the states in Europe whose political structure would become centralized and more fixed during the Renaissance period, as opposed to Italy, which was still fragmented by the end of the 16th century. The Reformation is usually considered the main reason behind the political centralization and the newly-assumed role of the monarchy in England. With the adoption of Anglicanism—a religious and political tool crafted by Henry VIII to escape the papacy's influence—the monarchy's position was stronger than ever. From the mid-16th to the early 17th centuries, the strength of the Crown allowed the cultural movement in England to prosper, but differently from Italy, Germany, and the Netherlands. The English Renaissance is now mostly remembered not for its visual arts but for its literature and drama.

The emergence of literature as the central aspect of the cultural heritage of the Renaissance in England was due to a widely-accepted notion that God's greatest gift to humanity was the tongue. Figures like Roger Ascham, a writer and the tutor to young Princess Elizabeth I, defended this idea and urged the masses to educate themselves to read and write properly. It came in handy that by the 1500s, the printing press had already found its place in the biggest cities and universities throughout England, making the spread of literary texts much easier. Moreover, with the new translations of the Bible from Latin or Greek into vernacular English, more and more people were interested in buying books—a direct effect of the Reformation. Thus, literature would flourish during the English Renaissance, shifting from medieval traditions to a more humanistic approach to literature in which more fiction books were being written. Owing to the rediscovery of ancient Roman and Greek texts, many of which were legendary plays by authors like Sophocles or Aristophanes, playwriting also emerged as a great part of this revival.

At the forefront of English Renaissance literature is none other than William Shakespeare, considered the greatest playwright of all time. Shakespeare's plays are a testament to his mastery of language, depth of characterization, and exploration of universal themes. His works, such as *Romeo and Juliet*, *Hamlet*, and *Macbeth*, continue to be performed and studied around the world. The appeal of Shakespeare comes from the fact that his plays are entertaining. Following the humanist tradition, his work demonstrates deep insights into human nature, love, power, and the complexity of human existence. Characters are fully fleshed out, with distinct personal qualities, engaging in interesting dialogues with each other that prove Shakespeare's abilities as a great playwright.

Another influential figure in Renaissance theater was Christopher Marlowe. Marlowe's work challenged the conventions of the time, bringing a darker and bolder style to the stage. His most famous play, *Doctor Faustus*, dealt with ambition, temptation, and the consequences of morally questionable decisions. Marlowe's plays are known for their intensity, poetic expression, and complex character exploration.

In addition to drama, poetry played an important role in Renaissance literature. Edmund Spencer's epic poem *The Fairy Queen* is considered a monumental work of the period. Celebrating the virtues of chivalry, love, and honor, it weaves together a complex narrative that blends allegory, myth, and history. Spencer's poetry became the defining work of English literature, testifying to his mastery of language and poetic imagery.

The rediscovery of ancient drama and the creation of new works by local artists inspired the establishment of theater culture in England more than in any other European country. Public theaters such as The Globe became centers of artistic expression, attracting people from all walks of life, including the aristocracy and the emerging middle class, and reflected the changing social and political conditions. Theater stages served as platforms for exploring complex issues and ideas, often challenging traditional beliefs and values. A wide variety of genres were popular, including tragedy, comedy, history, and romance.

The development of theater culture only increased the popularity of contemporary writers and playwrights. Shakespeare's works, for example, crossed borders and appealed to a wide range of audiences; they were even translated into different languages in the 1700s. Exploring themes of love, power, politics, and humanity with unprecedented depth and complexity, his plays were staged in open-air theaters where audiences could witness the spectacle of live performances, experience shared emotions, and gain collective catharsis.

English Renaissance theater culture was not confined to London but spread across the country. A company of actors toured different cities, bringing the magic of the stage to different communities. The spread of theater made it possible for people of diverse backgrounds to engage in the arts, contributing to the democratization of culture. The rise of English Renaissance theater also brought about the formation of theater groups and the emergence of famous actors. These actors have become cultural icons who embody the characters and emotions portrayed on stage. Theater was so popular that it became an integral part of the social fabric of the time, attracting audiences from all walks of life.

In conclusion, the renewed interest in classical learning and an appreciation for human potential were central humanist themes the English Renaissance shared with the movement in other places throughout Europe. However, the Renaissance in England can still be considered vastly different from the Northern and Italian Renaissances. The Italian Renaissance focused on art, architecture, and sculpture. The masterpieces discussed earlier exemplify the artistic achievements of the era. In contrast, the English Renaissance prioritized literature and drama, with playwrights and poets becoming cultural icons of the time instead of sculptors or painters. Moreover, the Renaissance styles of Italy and Northern Europe represented more secular worldviews, fascinated by the beauty and harmony of the physical world. Beginning with the depiction of religious themes, the movement matured to the expression of realism in everyday life or the glorification of human ideals in Mannerist paintings. In contrast, the English Renaissance retained strong ties to religious themes and moral considerations, as seen in the moral dilemmas explored in the works of John Donne and Shakespeare's plays.

Another important difference is the socio-political context in which these Renaissance periods occurred. The Italian Renaissance was supported by wealthy patrons such as the Medici family and later the Church, who support artists and scholars financially and intellectually. The Northern Renaissance owes its flourishing to the patronage of members of different social classes. In contrast, the English Renaissance featured the emergence of a middle-class audience that actively participated in theatrical culture, transforming theater into a more inclusive and accessible form of entertainment. Yet it would not have been as impressive without the support of the Crown, which contributed many resources to developing the cultural heritage so celebrated today.

Chapter Seven – The End of the Renaissance

Colonization

The history of the end of the Renaissance is complicated. This is mostly because we cannot definitively identify a single point when the Renaissance was no more. If nothing else, the whole history of the movement demonstrates that the Renaissance was not something with a definite starting and ending point: the social, political, economic, and cultural developments that took place from the late 14th to the 16th centuries were all deeply fused with each other. In addition, though we will later examine the end of the Renaissance in terms of the ceasing of artistic and intellectual progress, it can be argued that the Late Renaissance directly gave way to the Age of Enlightenment. Indeed, the advancements in political, economic, and scientific thought characteristic of Europe (especially of France, Britain, and Germany of the 17th-18th centuries) can be seen as direct consequences of the renewed will to learn and explore the world, which began with the Renaissance. Still, when we speak of the decline of the Renaissance, we usually mean the economic and political downfall of the Italian Peninsula in the 1500s— the place most associated with the Renaissance. Thus, now we will examine what caused the troubles and instability in Italy (and, to a lesser extent, the rest of Western Europe) that contributed to the traditional concept of the decline of the Renaissance by the end of the 1500s.

The beginning of the age of colonization can certainly be considered one of the factors that indirectly affected the decline of Italy as the cultural and economic center of Europe. Interestingly, the drive to colonize partially resulted from the development of Renaissance thought. We have mentioned that humanism stressed the importance of self-realization and humans' innate ability to master nature, which resulted in scientific and technological progress. One such technological development that revolutionized the way things were perceived at the time was the perfection of the design of caravels—smaller-sized, fast, and highly maneuverable sailing ships that allowed sailors to explore new maritime frontiers. Meanwhile, in the mid-15th century, due to the expansion of the Ottoman Empire and its blockade of Eastern trade by control of the southern Mediterranean, Europe needed to rediscover new trade routes. The Italian city-states of Genoa and Venice had monopolized the influx of trading goods from Asia in the Mediterranean, giving them an unfair advantage over merchants from France, England, or Iberia. Northern trade routes were also less developed at this time, as political troubles in Russia had destabilized the region and disallowed the establishment of reliable trade routes to Europe through Russia.

Thus, as a new way to circumvent the barrier of the Ottoman Empire was needed, the brightest and most creative minds of Western Europe started to look to the West instead of the East. Portugal and Spain would lead Europe in the endeavor to discover new trade routes to Asia. In the late 1400s, these powers gradually started to sail their way down the West African coast, discovering less civilized peoples and establishing trading outposts. A growing sense emerged that there was much to be explored to the south and especially to the west. In 1492, the infamous voyage of Christopher Columbus aimed to prove exactly that. Columbus, an experienced sailor and curious explorer from Genoa, believed that the rich Asian continent could be reached by sea if one traveled far enough to the west since it lay in the east. Technically, Columbus was correct—he had correctly identified the spherical shape of the Earth. However, due to the limited knowledge of geography outside of Europe at the time, he underestimated the size of the Earth. He had no idea that a huge landmass—which we now call the Americas—existed between Europe and Asia. Still, Columbus put his ideas into practice, obtaining funding and resources for an expedition from the Spanish Crown in 1492. But, as everyone knows, he did not reach India as he had imagined he would. Instead, Columbus landed on the Caribbean islands in October 1492, incorrectly identifying it as India and incorrectly dubbing the local American population Indians.

Thus began the age of colonization, which would transform the fate of European civilization forever. Establishing a reliable way from Spain to America, Columbus organized four expeditions, exploring the Caribbean basin and the eastern coast of Central America. Nobody had known that a landmass existed there, even though Europeans had, in fact, reached the place centuries before Columbus. Viking explorers led by Leif Eriksson had ventured all the way to Newfoundland around 1021. Unable to establish a foothold so far away from their home, they had abandoned their settlement. Knowledge of this legendary achievement had, of course, been lost in medieval Europe, so Columbus' discovery was a huge deal. Eventually, though Columbus firmly thought he had found a western route to India, Europeans realized that a whole new continent had been accidentally discovered and proceeded to explore it. What they found in the first decades of the 1520s were full-fledged civilizations in Central, North, and South America. The Europeans were able to easily overpower them with technological superiority. The Aztec, Maya, and Inca civilizations were tragically wiped out throughout the next few decades. The Europeans brought many communicative diseases for which the Native Americans had not developed immunity due to millennia of isolation.

Taking over the territories of the Native Americans, which were rich in natural resources and full of exotic foods, reliable trade routes were slowly established by Portugal and Spain—the two earliest and most successful players in colonization. These powers sent more and more exploratory missions to America to claim the lands in the name of their sovereigns and establish permanent settlements with permanent links to the European continent.

However, the influx of gold, silver, tobacco, and other extremely valuable trading goods into Europe by the mid-16th century came as a direct hit to the economies of the Italian city-states, which had never engaged in colonization mainly due to the lack of resources available to the centralized monarchies of Iberia and later France, England, and even the Netherlands. Economic decline was accelerated by the discovery of maritime trade routes to India by Portuguese explorer Vasco da Gama, which only increased the economic influence of Portugal in the Atlantic and Indian oceans. Soon, the once-great Italian city-states of Genoa,

Venice, and Florence were greatly challenged by the new players in international trade, and their excessive wealth gradually declined.

Trade patterns and economic focus would thus shift away from Italy, meaning that the old patrons of the Italian Renaissance culture no longer had means of financing the projects of Italian artists. Meanwhile, the Church's role as a patron also diminished with the Reformation. As the papacy invested more funds in fighting the spread of Protestantism, fewer resources were given to artists to continue creating the magnificent works characteristic of the High Renaissance, for example. Less demand resulted in less overall quality, and the subsequent drain of artistic and intellectual talent accelerated the decline of the Renaissance in Italy—at least compared to its previously amazing cultural output.

Political Factors

Finally, a series of troubles caused by political instability slowly had a snowball effect on the cultural output characteristic of the High Renaissance. We remarked in the beginning that, though they enjoyed a period of prosperity, Italian city-states were weak relative to the larger kingdoms beyond the Alps. The Ottomans also increasingly pressed in from the East, having finally defeated the Byzantines in 1453, and would reach the peak of their power in the next century or so. The Peace of Lodi, signed in 1454 by Venice, Florence, and Milan, was an agreement to come together if any of them were attacked by the Turks or the French—the two powers perceived to be the biggest threat to the Italians' sovereign interests. The treaty was upheld for the next four decades or so, and political turmoil was avoided in Northern Italy. However, it would not be long before their inner quarrels would render the whole system useless and lead to a period of political decline.

By the end of the century, however, Italy became a battleground for perhaps two of the strongest Catholic factions in Europe—France and the Holy Roman Empire. Following the absorption of the kingdom of Burgundy (which was primarily French) into the Holy Roman Empire, relations between the Habsburgs and the French kings started to deteriorate. To retaliate for losing his influence on Burgundy, King Charles VIII of France launched an invasion into Italy and press the claim he had on the throne of Naples. Aided by the Sforza family of Milan, which had had strenuous relations with the southern Italian state for a long time, Charles invaded Italy in 1494 with about 30,000 men. Naples, on the other hand, allied with the Papal States and Florence, both of which had the common interest of keeping the French out of the peninsula. For Florence, the domination of the French would mean the end of economic freedom and prosperity. Pope Alexander VI, however, a member of the infamous Borgia family, knew very well of the troublesome past of the papacy under the influence of the French kings during the 1300s and the dubious situation the so-called "Avignon papacy" period had caused for the Catholic world.

However, the Italian coalition was not nearly strong enough to stop Charles, whose army included professional mercenary infantry from Switzerland, considered among the best in Europe, and Scottish longbowmen. He defeated what the Italians had to offer relatively quickly. Seeing their armies defeated, the Medici offered the French control of Pisa in exchange for keeping them out of Florence. This act was perceived as treacherous by the Florentine republicans, who had long protested the despotic rule of the Medici. They thus overthrew the ruling family after about sixty years of rule and established the Great Council as the new main legislative body of the city—the same one that commissioned *David* to Michelangelo. King Charles would continue his devastating march south but was eventually repulsed from the Italian Peninsula by the Holy Roman Emperor and King Ferdinand of the Crown of Aragon—soon to be the king of Spain.

In the late 1490s, the political instability in Florence would become unfathomable as Savonarola—the chaotic and ambitious friar we mentioned briefly—took control of the city, resulting in his excommunication by the pope. For a brief time, Savonarola's influence reduced Florence to an ambiguous theocratic republic—or the closest thing to it—before the revolutionary was denounced and murdered by the Florentine citizens in 1498. Just one year later, the French returned to Italy, this time under King Louis XII, whose main aim was to capture Milan. He was aided in this endeavor by the papacy. What complicated the situation even more was the passing of Pope Alexander VI in 1503. The Borgia family lost control of the papacy, and the new pope, Julius II, was not so keen on keeping the alliance with France. The Frenchmen were defeated by the Spaniards once again, with the Spanish Crown, then controlled by the Habsburgs, claiming the throne of Naples for good. The year 1512 then saw the Medici rise to power in Florence once again with the help of the Spanish, and the French were driven out of Milan. In 1515, France recaptured Milan, but Charles I Habsburg of Spain (who was also Charles V of the Holy Roman Empire) would finally defeat the French in Italy in the 1520s.

The long wars weakened the Italian city-states beyond the possibility of recovery. Only Venice resisted German or French domination, but it was also slowly losing its former might due to the influx of goods from the New World into the markets of Europe. More fundamentally, the Italian nobility, largely replaced by the wealthy merchant class since the turn of the 14th century, started to regain their former power, returning to prominence in some cities. Even when the Medici again regained control of Florence in 1530, the art that was being produced no longer reflected the glory and optimism that had characterized the High Renaissance in the city. Many people recognized the drawbacks of the lack of a centralized political structure in Italy, which had become a battleground of foreign armies. Niccolò Machiavelli had laid this out the best in his 1513 work *The Prince*, which recognized the need for a strong ruler to rally the quarreling city-states to unite Italy and reach the old glory of Rome. A Renaissance work at its core, *The Prince* is Machiavelli's reflection on the political history of Italy and his lamentation of it, as well as his proposal for what it could have been. He posited his principles based on ancient writers such as Cicero and used historical examples to support his arguments.

Still, despite the public perception of the political situation, Italy suffered even more humiliation in the 1520s, as already mentioned. As a final nail to the coffin, Charles V's armies sacked Rome in 1527, at a time when the Catholic Church had already suffered immensely due to the turbulent processes begun with the Reformation. By then, the impulse of the Renaissance, born (or reborn) in the Italian Peninsula, was well on its way north, beyond the Alps. Though the movement had effectively ended in Italy, with only Venice, the city of Titian and Giorgione, maintaining its status as the center of artistic life, the Renaissance was alive for another century in the rest of Europe, producing a cultural heritage that has become invaluable today.

Conclusion

The Renaissance remains among the most influential periods in European history. With it came a great series of changes that altered the fundamental way life was perceived in Western Europe. Through an intellectual, artistic, and cultural rebirth, it ushered Europe out of the shadows of the Middle Ages and into an age of innovation, exploration, and enlightenment. It was a time of great curiosity and thirst for knowledge. The rediscovery of classical literature and advances in humanist philosophy ignited a passion for learning and set off a wave of scientific, artistic, and literary achievements that have transformed society. Leonardo da Vinci, Michelangelo, Galileo Galilei, Shakespeare, and other great men of their time revolutionized their fields and left an indelible mark on the world. Renaissance art captured the essence and undying spirit of human existence and embodied the ideals of the time. This ambition was expressed in sculpture, painting, architecture, and literature. Building on the brilliant heritage of classical antiquity, the quality of the culture during the Renaissance is often regarded as the pinnacle of European civilization.

The Renaissance also reassessed society and its values. Humanism emphasized personal worth, worldly knowledge, and human achievability. This era drove advances in anatomy, astronomy, and mathematics that questioned long-held beliefs and paved the way for a more rational, empirical worldview. The printing press invented by Johannes Gutenberg enabled the mass dissemination of this knowledge, leading to the democratization of information and the birth of the modern publishing industry. Spreading across Europe, stimulating cultural exchange and encouraging new ideas, the Renaissance should not only be considered an Italian movement. Its legacy continues to this day, and its influences can be seen in the principles of democracy, human rights, and the pursuit of knowledge that underpin the modern world. The Renaissance represents a period of transition and renewal in which the seeds of modernity were sown and continue to thrive.

For these reasons, when we look back on the Renaissance, we will always remember what it stood for—the indomitable human spirit always striving for perfection and improvement, the desire for mastery and a better understanding of nature, and the transformative impact of art and culture. The Renaissance continues to be a testament to humanity's ability to shape its destiny and create a brighter future through breakthroughs in thought and the undying curiosity that emerges from it.

Here's another book by Enthralling History that you might like

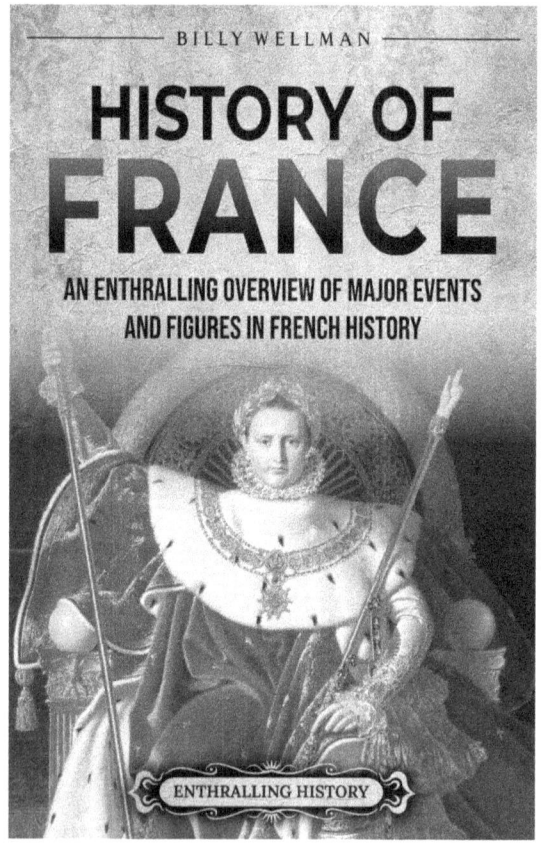

Free limited time bonus

Stop for a moment. We have a free bonus set up for you. The problem is this: we forget 90% of everything that we read after 7 days. Crazy fact, right? Here's the solution: we've created a printable, 1-page pdf summary for this book that you're reading now. All you have to do to get your free pdf summary is to go to the following website:

https://livetolearn.lpages.co/enthrallinghistory/

Once you do, it will be intuitive. Enjoy, and thank you!

Sources

Ackerman, J. S. (1998). Leonardo Da Vinci: Art in Science. *Daedalus, 127*(1), 207-224. http://www.jstor.org/stable/20027483

Bartlett, K. R., & Bartlett, G. C. (2019). *The Renaissance in Italy: A History.* Hackett Publishing Company.

Manca, J. (1995). Michelangelo as Painter: A Historiographic Perspective. *Artibus et Historiae, 16*(31), 111-123. https://doi.org/10.2307/1483500

Marrow, J. H. (1986). Symbol and Meaning in Northern European Art of the Late Middle Ages and the Early Renaissance. *Simiolus: Netherlands Quarterly for the History of Art, 16*(2/3), 150-169. https://doi.org/10.2307/3780635

Merriman, J. M. (2010). *A History of Modern Europe: From the Renaissance to the Present* (Third). W.W. Norton.

Müntz Eugène. (2019). *Michelangelo.* (A. Borges, Trans.) (Ser. Temporis collection). Parkstone International. Retrieved May 22, 2023, from https://public.ebookcentral.proquest.com/choice/publicfullrecord.aspx?p=6006696.

Müntz Eugène. (2019). *Raphael (Ser. Essential).* Parkstone International. https://public.ebookcentral.proquest.com/choice/publicfullrecord.aspx?p=5930199.

Nash, & Nash, S. (2009). *Northern Renaissance Art* (Ser. Oxford history of art ser). Oxford University Press USA - OSO. from https://public.ebookcentral.proquest.com/choice/publicfullrecord.aspx?p=5751187.

Nauert, C. G. (2006). *Humanism and the Culture of Renaissance Europe.* Cambridge University Press.

Séailles Gabriel, & Leonardo. (2011). *Leonardo da Vinci*. Parkstone International

Sullivan, M. A. (2008). Bosch, Bruegel, Everyman and the Northern Renaissance. *Oud Holland, 121*(2/3), 117-146. http://www.jstor.org/stable/42712203

Wasserman, J. (2007). Rethinking Leonardo da Vinci's "Last Supper." *Artibus et Historiae, 28*(55), 23-35. http://www.jstor.org/stable/20067137

Whitford, D. M. (2016). Erasmus Openeth the Way Before Luther: Revisiting Humanism's Influence on "The Ninety-Five Theses" and the Early Luther. *Church History and Religious Culture, 96*(4), 516-540. http://www.jstor.org/stable/26382865

www.ingramcontent.com/pod-product-compliance
Lightning Source LLC
Chambersburg PA
CBHW070341010526
44107CB00004B/581